SHOW AND TELL

Representing and Communicating Mathematical Ideas in K-2 Classrooms

Linda Dacey and Rebeka Eston

Math Solutions Publications
Sausalito, CA

To Marie Crispen and the many other teachers and children who so willingly shared their ideas.

Math Solutions Publications
A division of
Marilyn Burns Education Associates
150 Gate 5 Road, Suite 101
Sausalito, CA 94965
www.mathsolutions.com

Library of Congress Cataloging-in-Publication Data

Dacey, Linda Schulman, 1949–
    Show and tell : representing and communicating mathematical ideas in
  K–2 classrooms / Linda Dacey and Rebeka Eston.
      p. cm.
    Includes bibliographical references.
    ISBN 0-941355-50-0 (alk. paper)
    1. Mathematics—Study and teaching (Primary)   I. Eston, Rebeka, 1958–
  II. Title.
  QA135.6 .D33 2002
  372.7—dc21

                               2002003566

Editor: Toby Gordon
Production: Melissa L. Inglis
Cover design: Leslie Bauman
Interior design: Joni Doherty
Composition: Argosy Publishing

Printed in the United States of America on acid-free paper
06 05 04 03 02 ML 1 2 3 4 5

A Message from Marilyn Burns

We at Marilyn Burns Education Associates believe that teaching mathematics well calls for increasing our understanding of the math we teach, seeking greater insight into how children learn mathematics, and refining lessons to best promote children's learning. Math Solutions helps teachers achieve these goals by providing professional development through inservice courses and publications.

Our publications include a wide range of choices, from books in our new Teaching Arithmetic and Lessons for Algebraic Thinking series to resources that link math and literacy; from books to help teachers understand mathematics more deeply to children's books that help students develop an appreciation for math while learning basic concepts.

Our inservice offers five-day courses, one-day workshops, and series of school-year sessions throughout the country, working in partnership with school districts to help implement and sustain long-term improvement in mathematics instruction in all classrooms.

To find a complete listing of our publications and workshops, please visit our Web site at *www.mathsolutions.com*. Or contact us by calling (800) 868-9092 or sending an e-mail to *info@mathsolutions.com*.

We're eager for your feedback and interested in learning about your particular needs. We look forward to hearing from you.

A DIVISION OF MARILYN BURNS EDUCATION ASSOCIATES

Contents

Preface

Five years ago, when we began writing *Growing Mathematical Ideas in Kindergarten*, we had no idea that we would learn as much as we did. It was a gift to us, to work so closely together, joining our different perspectives as we tried to unravel and make sense of what we saw and heard in Becky's classroom. Two chapters in that book, "Learning to Talk and Listen" and "Representing Mathematical Ideas," particularly transformed our understanding of the challenges involved in learning and teaching mathematics. We knew that we wanted to return to this work and to continue our collaboration.

This book is the result. We included a greater range of grade levels and classrooms in order to broaden our perspective and to probe more deeply into the ways in which mathematical representation and discourse supports the growth of mathematical ideas for primary students and their teachers. We focused the chapters on mathematical content to emphasize the importance of subject matter and to illustrate how "show-and-tell" can permeate the various strands in our curriculum.

Throughout this experience, we have tried to recognize the developmental and cognitive needs and ranges of young children. The conversations and representations we have chosen to illustrate our ideas are not meant to provide expectations for student work. Rather, they are viewed as examples of possibilities and purposes, as natural expressions of students' growing mathematical ideas. It is a privilege to use what students have shared with us as the backbone of this book.

Countless kindergarten, first-grade, and second-grade teachers have helped to inform our work. We have captured only a few of their ideas in these pages. The teachers' voices are authentic; they are of colleagues in Becky's school and of teachers with whom we have worked in professional development settings. We have included their voices, primarily within sections titled "Teacher Reflections," to honor and to make explicit the complex decisions teachers make to support their students' thinking.

At all times we have tried to keep two guiding questions in our thoughts: *Why do we ask students to represent and communicate their ideas? What purposes do these acts serve in the learning of mathematics?*

Satisfaction comes in many forms. The opportunity to continue our work together and to learn from others, while being embraced with the love and goodwill of our families, is again a gift. Once again, we learned more than we ever thought possible.

Acknowledgments

This book features stories and student work from a number of classrooms. Numerous colleagues, workshop participants, pre-service teachers, and children have informed our work. We are profoundly thankful for their time, insights, and contributions.

We must acknowledge the particular support and encouragement of four teachers: Marie Crispen, Melissa Hartemink, Lisa Seyferth, and Julienne Webster. In their willingness to explore new ideas with their students and to read various stages of the manuscript, they provided immeasurable help and insight. We also must thank Colleen Payne, an extraordinary art teacher who created the illustration of the parade, featured in Chapter 6, for our work with kindergarten students. We are grateful for her talent and perspective.

We thank our editor, Toby Gordon, for her interest in this project from its earliest inception, and both Toby and Marilyn Burns for their guidance. Once again, the many talented people at Math Solutions, and in particular, our production manager, Melissa Inglis, and our copy editor, Melissa Dobson, have added to the pleasure and satisfaction of this work.

1

Show and Tell
An Overview

What Do We Mean by "Show and Tell"?

Do you remember show-and-tell from your childhood? Having children bring a treasured object to school to share with their classmates is a time-honored tradition in many early-childhood settings. When originated, it represented one of the few times that students initiated learning in the classroom. By selecting the item to be shared, the students decided what their classmates would talk about.

Although it continues to offer an opportunity for young children to develop their language skills, within today's busy classrooms, this activity is often limited to a brief viewing of a selected treasure. Further, the focus is on one child only, and at times, competition about who has what is unwittingly instilled. In contrast, in this book, we use *show-and-tell* to refer to a way of teaching and learning. Ideally, as an instructional approach show-and-tell offers the benefits of the traditional activity without some of its built-in limitations.

A focus on showing and telling—the representation and communication of thinking—encourages children to construct ideas as they make sense of their world. It requires children to organize ideas for themselves and to present information to others. It provides them the opportunity to listen to and to learn from each other, to gain respect for one another as they participate in a learning community.

Unlike the traditional show-and-tell activity, which occurs on a schedule, in our conception of this approach children show and tell throughout their learning experiences. Rather than being limited to situations in which a single child presents to the whole class, children represent their ideas alone, in pairs, or in small groups. Similarly, they can express their thinking when working independently with the teacher or when interacting with a group of other students.

When the class works as a whole, the focus is not on any one child, but on the exchanges among the group. The discourse emphasizes student-to-student interactions. The teacher may facilitate or monitor the conversations, but she does not dominate or control the discussion.

This type of show-and-tell is particularly important to the teaching of mathematics. Too often, learners of mathematics are passive. They are given rules or examples that they can replicate, but often they are unable to use their mathematical skills to solve real-world problems. They rarely create mathematical ideas for themselves, but rather they depend on the expert—the teacher—for direction. Over time, they may come to believe that they cannot do mathematics themselves.

Recent reform efforts have emphasized a more active approach to the study of mathematics. As a result, many classrooms have adopted a hands-on exploration of mathematical ideas. Such activities are not sufficient, however, for the development of deep-seated knowledge and skills.

To make the most of mathematical inquiry, students must grapple with ideas, formulate questions, make and test conjectures, describe their methods, and justify their conclusions. These are the expectations when a show-and-tell approach is made central to the teaching and learning of mathematics.

How Do We Represent and Communicate Ideas?

Think of the route you take from your home to the local supermarket or to a friend's house. Can you visualize the right- and left-hand turns in relation to one another? Can you count the number of lights? Do you know the names of the streets? If you had a guest who needed directions, would you draw a map or provide written directions? If you were the one receiving the directions, which would you prefer? What if you purchased something that came with those famous words: "Some assembly required"? Would you attend most to the written instructions or to the drawings?

Some people have a strong preference for either visual or verbal directions. They might put together a bookcase from pictures provided, never reading one word of the written instructions. Others might never look at pictorial instructions, preferring to follow the accompanying written steps. Many people combine verbal and visual suggestions. In fact, written directions often contain references to visual cues, as in an instruction such as "Turn right after the big red sign." Similarly, maps often contain verbal information such as the names of streets or the mileage relative to a particular road. If asked, many people would probably choose to be given a combination of verbal and visual instructions, even though they themselves might be unable to provide them.

Research has provided sustained confirmation that the human ability to process verbal or visual information improves with practice. Recently, it has been suggested that the areas in our brains that perform such functions become enlarged as we increase our use of them, much like our muscles expand with exercise. Scientists studied a group of London taxicab drivers and found that after just two years on the job, the areas in the drivers' brains responsible for storing mental maps of places (the hippocampus), grew larger.

Schools tend to emphasize the verbal processing of information. Yet if our students are to be able to have the fullest understanding of ideas and to develop the widest access to learning, they need opportunities to develop a variety of ways to represent and communicate information. They should be able to use gestures, drawings, models, words, symbols, dramatizations, and manipulative materials to convey ideas. Through this variety, a deeper and broader understanding develops.

How Does the Show-and-Tell Approach Unfold in the Classroom?

Here is an example from a first-grade classroom. It is December, so the students are familiar with classroom expectations.

The students have been engaged in writing workshop. Pencils, papers, and folders are scattered about the classroom in a flurry of ongoing activity. The class stops to clean up before going to lunch, but three pencils remain on the floor. The teacher chuckles as she takes note of them, formulating her plans for math time. She points the wayward pencils out to the children and says, "It seems that we often find pencils on the floor during cleanup. Let's see if we can solve a problem about this after lunch."

When the children return from lunch, they gather in a circle around the easel. Together, they read the problem, written on a large piece of paper:

> I was cleaning up the classroom the other day. I found 5 pencils on the floor under the table. I found 6 more pencils next to the window. How many pencils did I find?

The problem (adapted from Kliman and Russell 1998) is reread as a whole class, to help emergent readers become familiar with the text. Then the teacher facilitates a conversation about the problem.

TEACHER: WHO CAN TELL US ABOUT THIS PROBLEM?
  BILLY: It's about pencils.
  KERRI: I found some pencils this morning.
  NICK: We found them in different places.
 SELENA: You have to put them together.
TEACHER: WHAT DO YOU MEAN BY THAT?
 SELENA: You have to put the ones from the table and the window together.
TEACHER: DO YOU FEEL READY TO WORK ON THIS PROBLEM?

As heads nod, the teacher distributes a copy of the problem to each student. There is plenty of white space on the paper, as only one problem is presented. The children disperse about the classroom. Some work alone, some work in pairs, and some in groups, at a round table. The teacher circulates to monitor students' work and to be available to those who need further support.

Though they may begin with concrete objects, the students are expected to represent their work on paper. Sami solves the problem by drawing. She draws five pencils, each separated by a line, on her paper. She then draws six more pencils, recounting the figures several times as she does so, to see if another pencil is necessary. Like many of us, she has some difficulty predicting how much space she will need.

When she finishes her drawing, she brings her paper to her teacher and says, "Here's my answer." Her teacher responds, "Oh, I see you've drawn some pencils. What did you find?" "Oh," Sami replies. "I need to count them." She quickly returns to her desk and counts the pencils, writing the numerals as she does so (see Figure 1–1).

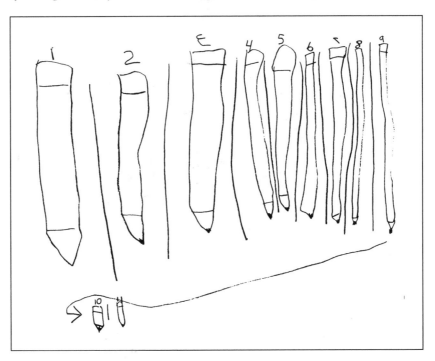

FIGURE 1–1   Sami's work

Nick takes his pencil and taps it across the table several times. Then he repeats the tapping, using his fingers to keep track of each tap. He records an 11 on his paper and brings it to his teacher. "It's eleven," he tells her as he shows his paper. When his teacher asks him to show how he got the answer, Nick draws the two groups of pencils and explains that he "just used his pencil" to get the correct sum (see Figure 1–2).

On their representations, Sarah and Zed each show an answer and indicate how they found that answer. Sarah (Figure 1–3) documents that she can use a known fact, 5 + 5, to find the sum of 5 + 6. It is clear from her representation that she used mental arithmetic rather than the manipulation of objects. Curious about the drawing, Sarah's teacher asks her what the dots above the figure's head mean. "Oh, that means I'm thinking it. It's sort of like a word bubble, but different."

FIGURE 1–2 *Nick's work*

FIGURE 1–3 *Sarah's work*

Zed uses small stones as models for the pencils. He forms a group of five stones, then six stones, and then pushes the two groups together. Next, he counts the stones one by one as he pushes them from one side of his desk to the other. In his representation (Figure 1–4), an arrow joins the two groups together.

While it is just midyear, the children are adept at showing their thinking and their answers. Sometimes the teacher asks a child if there is another way to show his work or record her thinking. Nathan records the equation 5 + 6 = 11. When the teacher asks him if he can show another way, he illustrates counting on fingers (see Figure 1–5).

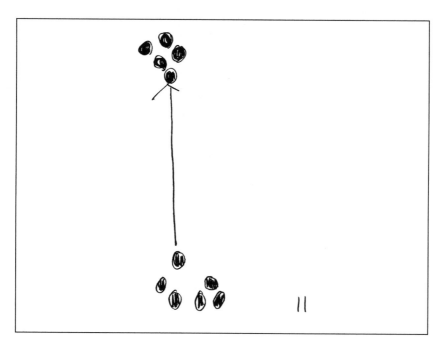

FIGURE 1–4   *Zed's work*

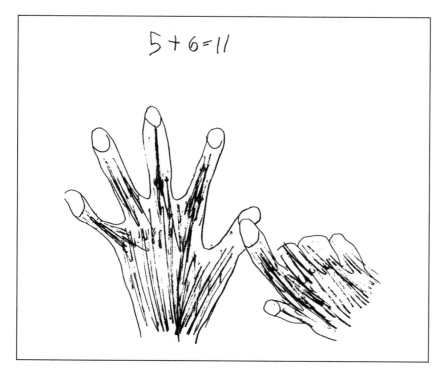

FIGURE 1–5   *Nathan's work*

Lucy's work (Figure 1–6), provides the greatest number of different ideas. She represents the pencils by drawing a single pencil labeled with a numeral that tells how many pencils are in each group. Her codes, "utt" and "btw," indicate which group is under the table and which is by the window. (The words are written out parenthetically after a classmate asks what the letters mean.) She draws hands another way to count the objects, and finally records the appropriate equation. She clearly has several ways to express her understanding of the problem and strategies for solving it.

The variety of these depictions is quite remarkable. These students have not been shown one right way to illustrate their work or answers. They have been allowed and encouraged to develop their own styles of pictorial and symbolic representation. Note that these representations can be thought of as both processes and products. That is, some children find the answer to the problem by making a representation of the given information. Other children may focus on the communication of their answer once they have found it. Some, like Lucy, portray an answer and a variety of ways to find the answer.

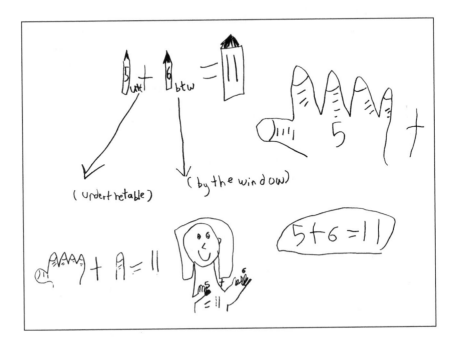

FIGURE 1–6   *Lucy's work*

Once the children have had the opportunity to record their work, they gather again in a circle to discuss their thinking. The teacher is aware that all of the children have now arrived at the correct answer. She confirms this with the group and then quickly steers the conversation toward the variety of ways in which the children solved the problem. Each child holds up his or her paper and talks briefly about what is shown. The following discussion then ensues:

TEACHER: WHAT DID YOU NOTICE ABOUT THE REPRESENTATIONS?

SAMI: There were lots of pictures of pencils.

TSUNG: And hands.

MADDY: I like the way Nathan drew the fingers.

TEACHER: DOES ANYONE ELSE HAVE A COMPLIMENT TO GIVE?

PABLO: I like Sarah's thinking dots.

ANTHONY: Does it always go like that?

TEACHER: WHAT DO YOU MEAN, ANTHONY?

ANTHONY: Well, that "one more" stuff *[referring to adding 1 to an easier equation, such as 5 + 5 = 10, to get 11]*.

TEACHER: THAT SOUNDS LIKE SOMETHING WE SHOULD INVESTIGATE.

Verbalizing their work is an essential part of a show-and-tell approach. It helps children to clarify and solidify their thinking and exposes them to the thinking of others. Such exposure allows for the development of a broader and deeper understanding of topics. Over time, children may adopt one another's approaches for solving problems or representing work. In this class, a few of the students began to use Sarah's "thinking dots" to indicate that they used mental arithmetic.

These conversations, or debriefing sessions, often lead to other investigations. Anthony has raised an important question. Although the "doubles plus one" strategy has been discussed previously, its use is not yet clear to all of the students. It appears as if Anthony is now ready to reconsider the idea.

Throughout this process, show-and-tell serves a variety of purposes. Some initial telling takes place to help children familiarize themselves with the situation. Then the children do some work that involves representing, either mentally or physically, the mathematical situation. The representation brings ideas more clearly into focus and helps children to develop deeper understanding. It may serve as a way to translate the abstract into the concrete. As they work, children coach each other and share their thinking—"tell"—with others sitting nearby. More "showing" then takes place as they are required to record their answers and represent their thinking.

When they finish their work and gather again as a group, students both show and tell their thinking. Through this sharing, they can begin to link a variety of representations of the same idea. This linkage allows for more robust mathematical thinking. They may also refine their thinking as a result of the debriefing or want to revise their work.

The ways in which communication and representation can permeate children's investigations of a mathematical task are summarized in Figure 1–7 on the following page. Note that as students come to understand and work on a task, communication and representation are *processes* that support their investigations. In the debriefing stage, the focus is on *products*.

Better Teaching

A show-and-tell approach to teaching helps us be better teachers of mathematics and our students be better learners of mathematics. There are a number of ways that this approach can support these goals. For example, it can provide us with insights into what every one of our students is thinking. Such insights help us to identify students' strengths and weaknesses. They inform our teaching strategies and instructional plans. We can better identify a question to ask or a material to use. Over time, we can better stimulate and support the learning of each child.

A show-and-tell approach holds children accountable. They know they must document their thinking. Through this documentation, they often understand their thinking more clearly. They may develop a deeper understanding of their work and identify new ideas to pursue. They are also expected to listen to others respectfully. Through the exchange of ideas, they make connections among different approaches and representations.

When children are expected to show and tell, it is easier to document their learning. Opportunities to record anecdotal notes about student conversations abound. Artifacts of student

	Processes	**Products**
Understanding Task	Reading the problem/ task together	Personal understanding of task statement
	Talking about what it means	
	Connecting with the language of the task statement	
	Brainstorming strategies	
Working on Task	Dramatizing the implied action	Notes
	Building models	Models and drawings
	Sharing ideas with a classmate	
	Making drawings to show what happens	
	Creating mental representations of the situation	
	Coaching classmates	
	Guessing and checking with models	
	Using notation to keep track	
	Creating an equation	
Debriefing	Linking representations	Oral presentation
	Reflecting on work	Recorded representation of thinking
		Recorded answer
		Class poster of ideas

FIGURE 1–7   *Show-and-tell processes and products*

thinking are numerous. By examining these records over time, we can analyze student growth and share this information with parents and school officials.

Today, teachers often feel pulled in several directions. Many early-childhood teachers believe in a constructivist approach to learning and want to ensure that their students have the opportunity to gain meaningful mathematical ideas in a developmentally appropriate manner. This may mean a curriculum and style of teaching that emphasizes building understanding and making connections. At the same time, teachers want to make sure that their students are learning the skills that they need. Further, parental and state influences are placing an increased emphasis on accountability and proof of effectiveness. A show-and-tell approach can help meet the simultaneous challenges for understanding, skill development, and accountability (see Figure 1–8).

How Can Teachers Support the Show-and-Tell Process?

The role of teacher has changed. No longer is she the one with all the answers, nor is it necessary for her to model each step of a problem in order for her students to parrot their knowledge back in some way. Instead, the teacher needs to share the stage with

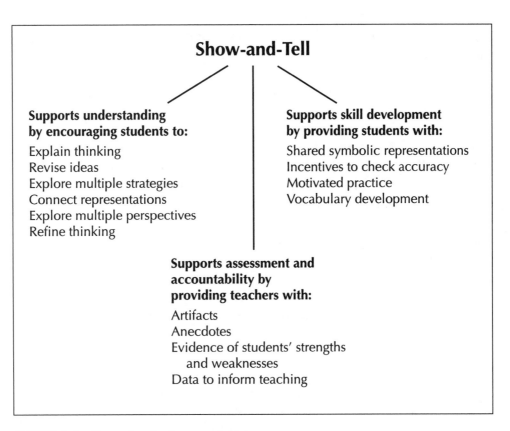

FIGURE 1–8 *Supporting simultaneous challenges*

her students. She needs to set the activity into motion and then step aside to see how her students make sense of each new situation. Her role varies daily, based on the needs of her students. In one situation she may act as a sounding board for a student trying out a hypothesis, in another she may need to ask probing questions to help students refine their ideas.

In the following conversation with a first-grade student, the teacher takes on the role of listener. Rosa has brought the book *The Bus Stop*, by Nancy Hellen, over to show her teacher. This book tells the story of people waiting in line at a bus stop. The characters are introduced sequentially, until seven people are in line. After each new person joins the line, a phrase is repeated—"But can you see the bus yet?" The facing pages at the end of the book show the seven people in line on the left page. The right page is a picture of a landscape. Embedded in the landscape are cutout rectangles. When this page is turned, the cutouts serve as windows on the bus. They are superimposed over the people standing in line, who now appear within the windows. The story has become a favorite in this class since it was read well over two weeks ago.

ROSA: Can I show you the trick in this book?
TEACHER: WHAT TRICK?
ROSA: You can see the bus, you know!
TEACHER: WHAT DO YOU MEAN?
ROSA: I'll show you. [*Rosa turns to the second-to-last page. The text reads, "Seventh is Ms. Pascal going to open her bookstore . . . but can you see the bus yet?"*] I can see the bus, can you?
TEACHER: NO.
ROSA: Look closely.

Though the teacher thinks she knows that Rosa is referring to the cutouts cleverly camouflaged in the illustration, she plays along as though she is not sure.

TEACHER: I DON'T SEE IT.
ROSA: Look, there are seven windows. [*She begins to count by running her finger over each of the cutouts that will become the windows on the bus when the page is turned.*]

ROSA: One, two, three, four, five, six. *[She counts again to make sure that she has counted correctly. It is clear that she is facing a mathematical dilemma.]* Wait a minute. There has to be seven!

TEACHER: WHAT DO YOU MEAN? WHY DOES THERE HAVE TO BE SEVEN?

ROSA: See *[she turns the page, revealing the red bus with the seven characters mentioned in the story seated, ready to drive away]*, there are seven. *[She counts out loud as she touches each person in the illustration.]* There are seven people. *[There is a long pause as Rosa carefully studies the illustration.]*

TEACHER: WHY DO YOU THINK THERE SHOULD BE SEVEN WINDOWS?

ROSA: There are seven people. Each person gets a window. *[Rosa continues to look critically at the picture.]* Oh, I get it! Sean and his mom are in the same window. He must have to sit with his mom because he is a baby.

During this exchange, Rosa stumbles upon a very important mathematical idea. As she begins to check her assumption of one-to-one correspondence, she discovers that there can be a two-to-one relationship as well. When a teacher can sit back and listen, innumerable possibilities may develop. Rosa's teacher has had the pleasure of witnessing this thinking evolve, and Rosa seems satisfied that she has shown her teacher the "trick" in the book. Indeed, Rosa has learned a new trick herself!

Teacher Reflection

I was so pleased that I had time to listen to Rosa. It's too often that one of the children comes up to me and I'm in the middle of something, too busy to really focus on what she is trying to tell me. The child knows I'm rushing, and therefore doesn't really take the time to fully communicate her ideas.

In order to support students as they engage in mathematical thinking, we need to see the value of giving them time to formulate their ideas. Time is needed as students tackle new concepts and develop representations that depict their thinking. Writing down a simple calculation takes considerably less time than showing how one arrived at a solution. Time must be provided so that students can continually build on their understandings and exchange their ideas.

In order for students to invest their time in this activity, they need to see the value of showing and telling their ideas. When we demonstrate a sincere interest in their thinking, students respond in kind. In effectively implementing the show-and-tell approach in our classrooms, many questions come to mind, including:

- Is there a best time or way for mathematical discussions to take place?
- What kind of representations can young children make? How do they change over the grade levels?
- How can we help young children stay engaged in this type of work?
- Can young children sustain a meaningful debriefing session?
- How can we use mathematical showings and tellings to inform our teaching and to assess learning?

This book focuses on the show-and-tell approach to teaching mathematics in kindergarten, first-grade, and second-grade classrooms. In order to help illustrate these techniques across the curriculum, chapters are organized around particular content strands. Throughout the chapters, classroom examples and teacher reflections shed light on the questions raised above.

2

Talking About Numbers

No one questions the importance of class discussions within the language arts or social studies curriculum. "Math talk," however, is still a relatively new idea. Initially, our mathematics curriculum didn't support conversations. Most of the tasks did not lend themselves to discussion or the sharing of ideas. Problems were usually given after skills had been learned by rote. The only task was to decide which rote skill to apply to which problem.

If children did speak when working on such tasks, it was to confirm the solution strategy or answer, or to alert a friend to the fact that he or she had made a mistake. So student-initiated conversation was limited to comments such as, "This is an addition problem, right?"; "Did you get nine?"; "That one's not right." Even when teachers asked questions to which they expected verbal responses, such questions usually required only a brief response. In fact, teacher-initiated talk was often in the form of questions such as, "What did you get for number 7?" and limited to numerical replies.

As our mathematical tasks have become more diverse and stimulating, there is more to talk about. Yet mathematical conversations are still risky for students and teachers alike (Dacey Schulman and Eston 1999). It is not easy to create a classroom in which children feel comfortable talking about their mathematical understandings. It is not easy for teachers to know how to support and facilitate this "telling" among young children. But if we are to have access to children's thinking and if children are to trust in their own knowledge, then our classrooms must become centers of mathematical discourse; they must be places where students are invited to "tell."

When teachers first introduce math talk into their classrooms, they are often delighted with the results. They are also frequently surprised by what their students don't know. Consider the comments of one teacher, who teaches second grade.

Teacher Reflection

I still remember the day when I first tried to engage my students in a mathematical conversation. I was taking a course and was required to reflect on a five-to-ten-minute class discussion. At the time, I was surprised at the assignment—after all, this was a course about teaching math. I was a bit nervous about the idea. What if I asked the students what they thought and no one said anything?

I decided to start with something that I was pretty sure would interest them. I showed them a teddy bear. At first we talked about what the bear's name should be. That was an easy way to begin; the children have had the experience of naming dolls, action figures, or stuffed animals of their own. Then I asked what we could measure about Brown Bear (our chosen name). The children were still eager to respond. As they gave ideas, I made a list of their suggestions.

It was delightful. Many of the children contributed to the discussion, and they were clearly listening to each other's ideas. My favorite response was the suggestion that we measure the bear's fluffiness after it was slept on. I knew right then that I wanted to have many more such conversations.

Next, I asked what we could use to measure the items on our list. To my surprise, no one suggested the use of standard measuring tools. Lengths and widths were to be measured "by arms," and weight by "picking (the bear) up to see." They wanted to compare the size of the eyes to the size of a penny. When I asked if a ruler would be helpful, one little boy responded, "What for?" I was very surprised. I had just assumed that rulers and scales would come to mind automatically. I didn't know what to do next. Should I tell them why it would be good to use a ruler?

A teacher's surprise is a common outcome of math talk. Such talk can take place throughout the day—from planned class discussions to informal conversations between two children. With teacher guidance, expectation, and encouragement, math talk can become a natural component of student interactions, which in turn supports the growth of mathematical ideas. These discussions also provide teachers with valuable insights into children's mathematical thinking.

Creating a Community of Learners

Class discussions provide students with a shared experience. When students relate their conjectures, arguments, and solutions, they are supporting each other as they form a community of learners. In such a community, students have many roles. They take on the role of teacher when they explain their methods or lead a conversation. They take on the role of audience when they listen actively to their peers' presentations. When they pose a question about what is said, compliment someone's work, or state a connection between the work of different students, they are in the role of critic or responder. With practice, students become adept at these various roles and soon recognize their importance.

Large-group conversations can occur at various points in an investigation or instructional sequence. Initially, such conversations serve as a way to launch a new topic or task. As a whole group, the class can share enthusiasm for an activity as well as gain common understandings. Talking about a task is a quick way to communicate ideas and brainstorm possible starting points.

Students are then ready to pursue their own inquiry. Depending on the activity, math talk may occur in pairs or small groups as children wrestle with the task and check their assumptions and findings. Some students may talk aloud as they work independently. This private verbalization seems to help some students to focus and keep track of their thinking.

Midway through an investigation may be another good point to bring the whole class together. This is a time for students to share their progress, to explain what they are doing and finding. Some students may need to hear what others are accomplishing to gain confidence in their own approaches. Other students may broaden their thinking as they learn about their classmates' different perspectives. Sometimes misconceptions are corrected when a student is questioned by others.

Such conversations often lead to the use of specialized terms. Students may repeatedly use the word *opposites* to identify addition expressions with switched addends, such as 3 + 9 and 9 + 3, *corners* to refer to angles, and *six-sided ones* for hexagons. Such terms have meaning for students and can later be connected to standard vocabulary. These connections occur easily when initial meaning is understood. Questions such as "Does anyone know another name for six-sided ones?" provide opportunities for students to identify standard terms. Teachers can also introduce standard terms with statements such as, "Some people call six-sided ones 'hexagons.'"

Final debriefing sessions provide students opportunities to report their findings. Such presentations help students to clarify their thinking and to summarize their ideas. Generalizations are often made and common vocabulary is reinforced. It is here that concepts and skills can be crystallized and strengthened. Questions such as "Is this always true?" may lead to new investigations.

Initially, students and teachers may not be skilled in discussions about mathematics. It takes time to learn to be an active, respectful, and responsive listener. Young children, just learning new ideas, may get frustrated trying to understand their classmates' thinking. But even young children are capable of mathematical discussions. Consider this example from a first-grade classroom in mid-September.

The teacher gathers the children in a circle and reads them the following verse.

> Numbers all around us,
> What places can you name?
> What do they tell us?
> Are they all the same?

The children repeat the verse many times and then the teacher asks, "Where do you find numbers?" After an initial silence, two students speak up simultaneously.

LAUREN: On cards.

ENRICO: Right there on the paper.

TEACHER: WHICH PAPER?

ENRICO: The one over there [pointing to a chart where the class was beginning to keep track of the number of days they have been in school].

TEACHER: WHAT ARE THEY FOR?

KATIE: The number of days.

TIA: [Pointing to the attendance chart.] And how many kids we have.

BRANDON: In books.

JAMAL: On the clock.

SAM: On your shirt [pointing to a classmate wearing a sport jersey].

TEACHER: WHY ARE THERE NUMBERS ON TANYA'S SHIRT?

LUKE: I think it is so they can tell them apart.

TEACHER: WHAT DOES LUKE MEAN BY THAT?

DENZEL: Like my soccer shirt number is seven and my sister's is twenty-three.

TEACHER: WHERE ELSE DO WE FIND AND USE NUMBERS? THINK ABOUT YOUR HOUSE.

OPAL: Your mailbox and phone.

BRANDON: On your door.

PATTI: An alarm.

KARLENE: On your driver's license.

TANYA: Your microwave.

BRANDON: If you press two thousand, it will cook for two thousand minutes.

JAMAL: Your license plate.

SAM: If you do a bad thing, the police can tell who you are.

LUKE: The temperature.

CARLITA: Your watch.

TIA: Cents.

The range and specificity of her students' examples impresses the teacher. She thinks the children could probably continue to list many possibilities, but she wants them to do some work on their own. She's learned that they can't sit too long in a class meeting without becoming restless and distracted. She asks the children to draw a picture of one of the places that numbers can be found. She thinks that after working independently, they will return to the discussion with new energy.

For the next fifteen minutes, the students make their drawings. Some students illustrate the idea that they had suggested in the discussion, some depict a classmate's suggestion, and some create new ideas. While the children are working, the teacher circles about the classroom, supporting students when appropriate. She notices that most of the children are drawing items such as computer keyboards, houses, mailboxes, and telephones, but that no one is depicting a number used to convey quantity. To give students an opportunity to consider this idea, she makes her own drawings. On one piece of paper she draws a crayon box, an item familiar to the children. She puts an 8 on the box to indicate that the box holds eight crayons. She then draws a carton of eggs and writes "1 Dozen (12 eggs)" on the side. She decides to introduce these drawings during the debriefing.

After the children finish their pictures, they return to the meeting area to share their work. The teacher is curious to see if the children can categorize their responses in some way. Might these first-grade students have the notion that numbers can be used in different ways? She invites the children to share their work in round-robin fashion. This technique helps start the conversation as it focuses on individual work. She also wants to set the expectation that everyone has an idea worthy to share. After everyone has a chance to speak she asks, "Are these numbers all used for the same thing?"

BRANDON: There are two clocks.

TEACHER: DID ANYONE ELSE NOTICE THAT? *[A few children nod their heads.]* MAYBE WE SHOULD PUT THE TWO CLOCKS IN THE CENTER OF OUR CIRCLE. *[The two children whose drawings are of clocks place their work inside the circle.]*

TEACHER: ARE ALL NUMBERS USED IN THE SAME WAY?
[The children are silent. The teacher waits, hoping that one of the children will respond in some manner. When there is no response, she tries a different approach.] ARE THERE OTHER IDEAS THAT GO TOGETHER?

MELISSA: You can put this watch with the clocks. *[She places her drawing of a watch with the clocks inside the circle.]* They are really the same.

LUKE: I have a number on a shirt. That's like Tanya's. *[Both children had drawn a sport jersey with a number on it.]*

TEACHER: LET'S PUT THESE TOGETHER. ARE THERE ANY OTHERS? *[Silence again. Though the children are not responding quickly, the teacher can see that they are intrigued. To continue the conversation, she brings out her drawings.]* I ALSO MADE SOME DRAWINGS. CAN YOU TELL WHAT THEY ARE?

ENRICHO: Yeah, that's the crayon box.

TIA: That one is for eggs.

TEACHER: WHAT ARE THE NUMBERS ON THESE TELLING US?

LUKE: Oh, I see, eight crayons, just like in our boxes.

CARLITA: And that has twelve eggs.

TEACHER: HOW ARE THESE NUMBERS THE SAME?

PATTI: It tells how many are in it.

JAMAL: They tell you how many you get.

TEACHER: IS THAT THE SAME AS OR DIFFERENT FROM THE TELEPHONE?

TANYA: The telephone just uses the numbers to dial. They don't really mean anything. You just dial.

TEACHER: DO YOU FOLLOW WHAT TANYA IS SAYING?

JAMAL: It's like a code on a lock.

TIA: But these numbers *[pointing to the crayon box and egg carton]* mean how many. These *[pointing to the clocks]* don't.

TEACHER: CAN YOU THINK OF OTHER THINGS LIKE THE CRAYON BOX?

KATIE: There are numbers on things at stores.

OPAL: They're on puzzle boxes. *[Opal gets up and retrieves a box top from a puzzle the children had been working on together. She points to "100 pieces" written on the box.]*

TEACHER: WHAT DOES THAT MEAN?

TIA: The number of pieces in the box.

PATTI: That's not true. There aren't really a hundred pieces.

TEACHER: HOW DO YOU KNOW THAT?

PATTI: We've been counting them. There are more than a hundred.

TEACHER: THAT'S INTERESTING. I DIDN'T KNOW THAT.

The discussion had gone on long enough, and the teacher knew that the children would soon get restless. She was satisfied that her students had begun to recognize that numbers are used in different ways. Though they had not categorized all of their responses, they had been able to decipher an important difference: numbers are used to quantify as well as to label in some way. The children who thought of a telephone number as a code understood that such a number was different than the 8 appearing on the crayon box. These are important distinctions, though subtle and complex for young children. By sharing their ideas and talking together, they were able to identify their emerging ideas.

It is clear that, throughout this conversation, the teacher had to decide when to intervene and how to do so.

How Can Teachers Support Student Conversations?

It can be difficult for teachers to remain silent. As a result, classroom conversations often follow a student-teacher-student-teacher response pattern. That is, one student speaks and then the teacher responds to that student. Then another student speaks and the teacher responds to him or her. In such a format, students are speaking to the teacher, but not to each other. They learn that they are not really expected to engage in the conversation; they learn to be passive. We must learn to get out of the way. Student discussion can be encouraged with questions such as, "What do the rest of you think about this idea?"; "Does anyone else have this idea?"; "Who can think of something that will help here?"

Over time, it is the students' comments that drive the discussion. The teacher's job is to ask questions to scaffold the discussion, allowing student comments to build on other student comments. Although teachers may decide to interject an idea, most teacher comments focus on process; the students' comments focus on content. In this way, the dialogue builds and the students are engaged in the meaningful exchange of ideas.

Many of us have developed the habit of correcting a student when he or she says something incorrect. This behavior maintains the teacher as the mathematical authority. It is far more powerful for students to correct themselves or to challenge one another. This allows all learners to gain mathematical authority, to be in the role of sense makers.

Sometimes a correction won't be made. It is difficult to let ill-formed or incorrect ideas stand. Yet, "telling the answer" rarely has the intended effect. Such answers are often not understood or quickly forgotten. It is usually better to think of a follow-up activity that will help students to readdress the situation. A comment such as, "I think we have more to investigate here; we'll come back to this idea tomorrow," alerts students to the fact that they haven't yet reached closure, without simply telling them what is right.

We need to learn how to best help the shy students in our classrooms. Debriefing sessions can be difficult for students who find it intimidating to speak in front of large groups. It can be beneficial to provide an opportunity for students to practice for these sessions. Some teachers have "rehearsals" in which students present their work in pairs in preparation for the debriefing session. Some shy students prefer to speak first, rather than waiting with trepidation for their turn. Other students may want only to show their work rather than describe it verbally. This type of representation allows them to participate in the debriefing process without having to speak much. Over time, their representations may stimulate questions to which they are comfortable responding.

Teachers also have to think about ways to keep more talkative learners from dominating conversations. While there are always some children (and adults!) who talk more than others, it is important that all students have the opportunity to speak if they so wish. Questions such as "Does anyone who hasn't spoken want to add anything?" invite others to speak without devaluing the contributions of a learner who is highly engaged in the conversation.

Ideally, each student recognizes his or her own importance in the sense-making process. As teachers, we can further this recognition by valuing all students' contributions. As suggested by Whitin and Whitin, "we must value their language, questions, descriptions, observations, and stories because these are windows into the process of how our students construct meaning" (2000, 2).

Engaging Tasks

Some tasks stimulate more conversations than others. Tasks that are overly familiar and whose solutions are readily apparent rarely provide students with something to talk about. Students are more likely to discuss tasks that encourage multiple perspectives and solution strategies. Sometimes tasks initially appear difficult to students. When they begin to discuss the task together, they find that they *do* have ideas and then they feel more confident beginning their work.

Fit the Facts problems provide a brief "story" with numerical information missing. Sometimes numbers are given from which the students must choose; sometimes all numerical choices are open to students. In either case, numbers must be inserted so that the completed story is reasonable—that is, the facts must fit. Such problems help to develop students' number sense.

In early November a second-grade teacher introduces a *Fit the Facts* problem to her class. In the initial large-group discussion, she asks her students what an activity with this name might involve.

CLAIRE: You have a box of numbers and there's different questions, like even and odd, and you have to cross off all the odd ones.

SANDY: A fact is sort of like . . . here's an example. A fact would be telling you like which state the Mississippi is in. A fact tells you about countries.

TEACHER: CAN SOMEONE ADD MORE TO WHAT SANDY IS SAYING ABOUT A FACT?

RUDI: A fact is something that is true.

MACKEY: And like Claire said, you get clues and clues and clues and you get to the number.

After this brief exchange the teacher shows the class an enlarged copy of the *Fit the Facts* problem (Figure 2–1). She encourages the children to follow along with her as she reads the directions and text. Once the students appear clear about the expectations, copies of the problem are distributed and children head off to complete the task.

As they work, the teacher moves around the classroom, watching and listening for emerging ideas or confusions. She hears Natasha (while pointing to the $1\frac{1}{2}$ on her paper) ask Rudi, "Is this one number or two?" Rudi replies that he thinks it is one number but that it means "one and a half." As the teacher moves away from these children she hears Rudi say, "I don't think she's forty-five or ninety-six. That's too old. She wouldn't be in grade two. If she was one and a half, she wouldn't be in any grade." Rudi then records 8 for Ling's age.

Next she hears Mackey mumble to herself, "One and a half doesn't make sense." Mackey is working on the clue about the

---

All About Ling

Use each number once.
Your story must make sense.

Ling is _____ years old.

She is in grade _____.

There are _____ children in her class.

Ling lives at _____ Maple Street.

She is _____ inches tall.

She lives _____ miles from school.

45	96
$1\frac{1}{2}$	24
8	2

FIGURE 2–1   *Fit the Facts problem*

number of students in Ling's class. She has already determined that Ling is eight years old and that she is in grade two. Mackey has written these answers on her paper and has circled the 8 and 2 in the box, presumably to remind herself that these numbers have already been used. The teacher asks Mackey why one and a half doesn't make sense. Mackey replies, "One child would have to be cut in half. And ninety-six doesn't make sense, that's way too big. Forty-five doesn't make sense either. It has to be twenty-four." Mackey records the answer on her sheet and then circles the 24 in the box.

Other rumblings and comments can be heard as these second-grade students continue to work. The students are comfortable engaging in quiet discourse with nearby classmates. Some students, who are working alone, occasionally talk aloud as they reason through the problem. Conjectures, confusions, and solutions emerge all around the room.

BRAD: In second grade, hmm . . . There isn't a 7 here, so she has to be eight.

JOEY: She has to be a grown-up if she has children in her class. She couldn't be eight.

SKYE: She's not one and a half inches tall—that's obvious.

LESLIE: [Speaking to Claire.] The only one that's easy is one and a half. I know that she can't be one and a half, and that isn't her grade.

CLAIRE: [To Leslie.] And there can't be one and a half kids in the class. But then what is one and a half?

TOMAS: We had twenty-four kids in our class last year. I think it's twenty-four.

After the children seem satisfied with their solutions, they gather for a debriefing session.

TEACHER: THIS WAS A NEW TYPE OF PROBLEM FOR OUR CLASS. DID YOU THINK THIS WAS HARD OR EASY? [The children overwhelmingly agree that the problem was challenging.]

RUDI: I really had to think a lot about the numbers.

CLAIRE: It was fun. It told a story with numbers.

TEACHER: HOW DID YOU BEGIN TO SOLVE THIS PROBLEM?

NADIA: I thought about how old she was. I know you can be eight in second grade, so I wrote eight.

UNA: But I'm seven, not eight.

TEACHER: WHAT DO OTHER PEOPLE THINK ABOUT THESE IDEAS?

BRAD: I'm seven, too, but I will be eight and still be in second grade. I think that's the only one that makes sense.

JOEY: I thought she was a grown-up.

TEACHER: DID OTHER PEOPLE THINK ABOUT THAT?

RUDI: I did. But I knew she had to be in second grade.

TEACHER: I NOTICED THAT AS SOME OF YOU WERE WORKING, YOU CIRCLED THE NUMBER WHEN YOU DECIDED WHERE TO USE IT. WHY DID YOU DO THIS?

RUTH: You could only use the number once. I didn't want to get confused, so I circled it when I used it.

TEACHER: WHICH ONE DID YOU DECIDE ON NEXT?

MURPHY: Twenty-four.

TEACHER: WHERE DOES THAT GO?

MURPHY: For the class.

TEACHER: WHY?

MURPHY: I don't know.

TOMAS: Last year we had twenty-four kids in my class.

TEACHER: DOES IT MAKE SENSE TO HAVE TWENTY-FOUR?

The class responds with a strong yes. A brief amount of time is then spent exploring the sense of having ninety-six, forty-five, or one and a half children in a class, but the children agree that none of these seem right.

TEACHER: WHAT DID YOU DECIDE NEXT?

LESLIE: Ling lives at ninety-six Maple Street.

TEACHER: HOW MANY PEOPLE PUT NINETY-SIX? *[Lots of heads nod in agreement.]* WHY DID YOU DECIDE THAT NINETY-SIX GOES THERE?

SKYE: Because most streets are really high numbers or really low numbers.

CLAIRE: I did a different one next. I decided that she was forty-six inches tall. Then how far she lives from school.

TEACHER: DID ANYONE ELSE SOLVE IT IN THIS ORDER?

TOMAS: Yes.

TEACHER: WHY DID IT MAKE SENSE TO START WITH HOW MANY INCHES TALL LING IS?

CLAIRE: Because it could've been any of those numbers for the street number.

RUDI: No. No one lives at one and a half Maple Street.

JOEY: That doesn't make sense.

UNA: That would be . . . that would be silly. No way! You can't have a half a house. No way.

MACKEY: You can have house A and house B. Like two houses in one. But they don't do house one-half.

NATASHA: We have that, in my apartment. But it's never one and a half.

LESLIE: I did one and a half miles from school.

TEACHER: WHY?

LESLIE: Because she couldn't live ninety-six miles away, that's why.

TEACHER: WHY NOT?

MACKEY: I don't even live a mile from school, that's why I have to walk. I don't get to ride the bus.

TOMAS: I think ninety-six miles is way too far.

CLAIRE: Plus, I used the forty-five for the inches tall.

TEACHER: WHY FORTY-FIVE?

BRAD: Because ninety-six doesn't make sense. It can't be ninety-six. It's way too big.

MACKEY: It's way too tall. The three that are left are forty-five and ninety-six and one and a half. I know that four feet is forty-eight inches and I'm four feet, so does it make sense that ninety-six inches could be her height?

LESLIE: Before I looked at the question, I counted myself by inches. *[Leslie shows that she took her thumb and pointer finger and spread them about an inch apart. She then demonstrates how she started at her heel and carefully measured how tall she was by moving her fingers up her body.]* I got about forty-five.

BRAD: For the inches, ninety-six inches is five feet.

TEACHER: THAT'S A CHALLENGE I'LL LEAVE FOR US TO FIGURE OUT ANOTHER TIME. IS FIVE FEET, NINETY-SIX INCHES?

JOEY: I don't think it's ninety-six inches, because inches are small.

As the teacher scans her class, she realizes that almost all of the children are trying Leslie's measurement strategy. Even though they had not completed the discussion of the *Fit the Facts* problem, they had been sitting for a long time engrossed in this conversation, and now it had sparked an additional mathematical investigation.

When students engage in meaningful discourse and exchange of ideas, countless opportunities for further exploration arise.

Teacher Reflection

I had no idea that such a rich discussion about numbers could take place in my second-grade class. When I first looked at this problem, I wasn't sure if the children would be able to make sense of the last three clues. I knew some children would naturally begin to talk with a classmate about their thinking. This is very much how I run my classroom throughout the day, regardless of what subject we are studying. I was delighted by how many children completed the task successfully, but even more so by the range of knowledge and logic they used when interpreting the use of the different numbers.

Needless to say, this session launched an investigation into measuring individual height. I had wanted to have the children measure how tall they were, but had not gotten around to it yet this year. Now we had the perfect reason to do so. Once the children used Leslie's measuring technique, they were surprised at the wide range of their findings. Children even started checking each other's heights. Since not all children formed the same distance between their thumb and index finger, this led to even greater variation. I wonder if this is a good time to talk about why we have standard units?

I have always had a large measuring tape on the back of the classroom door. Tomas decided that we should measure everyone and check whether ninety-six inches was really five feet, like Brad suggested.

I was amazed that Mackey knew that she was four feet tall. I later asked her about this, and she said she knew that there were twelve inches in a foot. Also, she had just gotten measured at the doctor's.

I realize that we did not come to closure on the problem during this debriefing session. The children were so taken by the measuring idea that I decided not to force their return to the original problem right at that moment. We did come back to it later in the day. The children seemed very proud that they had solved what they thought of as a challenge. I was proud, too.

As I reflect further on the conversation, I wish I had followed up a bit with Joey. I wonder what he meant about inches being small. Does he have a sense that when a unit of measure is small it takes more of them, than when compared to a larger unit? I'm not sure how to follow up on this now. Perhaps I can observe Joey more closely as we begin to measure other types of objects.

This conversation demonstrates how students can learn to talk in large groups with limited teacher direction. These second-grade students shared solutions along with their reasoning as they listened to both each other and the teacher. They compared strategies, gained confidence, and became interested in new ideas. Children can also lead their own conversations.

Student-Led Conversations

It is not necessary that mathematical conversations be led by a teacher. There are a variety of ways in which students can lead discussions or activities. Many classrooms have "leaders of the day" who are responsible for morning calendar and attendance activities. Such leaders help their classmates to determine who is present, to identify the date, and to complete other classroom rituals.

Students can also emcee games. For example, a student can think of a number and then call on students to ask "yes or no" questions enabling them to guess the number. Within this role, students learn to negotiate correcting their peers with replies such as "That's not a yes or no question." They learn to respond to classmate complaints such as "You never call on me. I was going to guess that number." Some classrooms discuss the role of emcee and the issue of fairness. For example, one classroom created a "side, middle, other side" rule. The rule requires the emcee to call on a student on one side of the room, then in the middle, then on the other side. Some classes require that a boy be called on after a girl.

Students can also lead mathematical activities that they have prepared themselves. One second-grade classroom has a traveling estimating jar. When a student is the leader of the day, she takes the estimating jar home that night. Her job is to fill up the jar with small items (pennies, paper clips, marbles, blocks) from home. She counts the items as she places them in the jar. The next day she brings the jar to class and says, "I have filled the jar with [name of item]. How many items do you think are in the jar?"

The children write their estimates on Post-it notes. For the first few times this activity is conducted, the teacher invites students to place their Post-its on a number line at the front of the room, by asking questions such as, "Did anyone estimate in the twenties?" Those students answering in the affirmative bring their Post-its to the front of the room and place them along the number line. When all the Post-its are on the line, the student leader announces how many items are in the jar and the students identify the estimates that are closest to the correct amount. After a few "modeling sessions," the student leader can be the one to ask the questions that result in students placing their estimates on the number line.

Young students also lead simple mathematical conversations among themselves as they play. In many kindergarten classes, manipulative materials are made available to students during what might be called choice time, or exploration time. One day in late fall, two kindergarten students show interest in a set of "kid counters" (similar to teddy bear counters, these materials are small plastic figures of people used for counting, classification, and patterns). The children also want to use dice. Spurred by a desire to explore these materials, they invent what seems to be a counting game for themselves. During their exchange of ideas, they solve several problems together. Their conversation is

lively and a genuine sense of friendship and playfulness under-
lies their collaboration.

SABRINA: Let's put the people in the middle. *[Sabrina scoops out a handful of kid counters and places them in the center of the table. She is sitting on one side; Jordi is on the other.]*

JORDI: Yeah, now I can role the dice. *[Jordi roles the two dice and gets a 4 on each one.]*

SABRINA: Now move one.

Jordi takes one of the kid counters from the pile and seemingly at random counts aloud from one to four as she bounces
the piece in her hand along the table. She then repeats "One,
two, three, four" with a similar action and lands the piece at an
unmarked resting place on the table.

SABRINA: Now it's my turn.

Sabrina roles the dice and also gets a 4 and a 4. She takes a
kid counter from the center of the table and counts out one
through eight as she moves the piece and then lands it. Again,
these actions seem random, though Sabrina appears deliberate.
There is no board for this game, or marked-off spaces on the
table. Sabrina finishes her count and passes the dice to her
friend.

JORDI: I got a six and a two. *[Jordi takes a new piece and counts aloud, "One, two three, four, five, six" and then "One, two" and lands her new piece. She passes the dice to Sabrina.]*

Sabrina roles a 3 and a 2. She takes a new piece and counts
aloud from one to ten.

JORDI: Uh-oh. You moved ten. That's too much.

SABRINA: Oh yeah, two and three is five. Five and five are ten.

Sabrina takes the same piece she just moved and counts
aloud from one to five.

Neither Jordi nor Sabrina seem bothered by this extra move, or the friendly correction. Jordi now roles a 3 and a 1. As she begins to move a third piece, Derix walks by the table where the girls are playing. He looks at the dice and says, "One and three is four," then he walks on. Jordi takes her new piece and counts "One, two three" and "One."

Teacher Reflection

I try to have lots of opportunities where children can use their own ideas and interests while at work and play. I noticed that Jordi and Sabrina had taken out the kid counters and some dice. This was not the first time I had seen this duo select these materials. I didn't want to interfere in their game, their learning, so I watched from afar. I chuckled as they counted out each move. Was there a point to this game? It didn't seem to matter.

I noticed that Jordi seemed to need to count each separate move. She seemed to recognize the amount of dots on the die, but did not join them together in any way. Sabrina did have a way of joining numbers. I'm not sure if she was counting on from one of the numbers, or just knew some facts, or could count quickly in her head.

I thought it was interesting when Jordi corrected Sabrina. I love to see children work things out together. This was obviously not a problem, just something needing correction.

I also chuckled when Derix interjected his fact knowledge. Jordi didn't seem to be swayed by this in how she performed her turn, or by the way Sabrina counted out her moves.

I don't know if the girls even noticed that I was watching them. I try to be invisible as I observe, so that I can witness natural conversations. Although I know there are times when I need to interject, I also know that if I comment, my interference becomes dramatic. Soon students are talking to me and not to each other.

I'm not always sure what to do in moments like these. Should I ask the girls to teach other classmates their game? Should I let them take on that role naturally if other kids show an interest? Should I include other board games in our choice time selections?

The conversation between these two friends was simple, yet rich. I hope to facilitate more conversations like this in my class. I don't mean by being the leader of the discussion, but by giving children time, choices, and appropriate opportunities to create their own dialogue and debate together.

Whether it takes place in whole class, small group, pairs, or through individuals verbalizing their thinking, math talk gives teachers access to student thought processes. It also exposes the delightful nature of students' ideas. It gives students the opportunity to participate in mathematical dialogue, to express their ideas, and listen to the thinking of others. These conversations build on the intuitive understandings that children bring to school. They help children think of themselves as people who can talk and reason about mathematics.

3

Connecting Numbers, Stories, and Facts

When many of today's teachers were students in school, an operation such as addition was practiced until it was mastered, and only then was it applied to the solution of story problems. There was no particular mathematical challenge in solving problems listed under a heading, such as, "Using addition to solve problems," but that was how it was done. Once skill in more than one operation was developed, there was mixed practice that required students to "Choose the operation to solve the problem." Few kindergarten and first-grade classrooms focused on story problems very much, and even problems considered in the upper elementary grades had a predictable syntax and format.

In many classrooms today, story problems are introduced much earlier. Rather than at the final stage of learning an operation, children in kindergarten can be introduced to story problems as one initial step in the formal study of arithmetic. Their natural curiosity and intuition lead them to construct their own techniques for solving such problems. Over time, with the representation and communication of their thinking, these problems can become connected to arithmetic techniques and number sentences.

At the kindergarten level, the focus is on children learning to make sense of problem situations. Early work emphasizes modeling the problem. Students may act out the problem themselves or manipulate objects. The type of object manipulated is very important. What is concrete versus abstract may differ from child to child and from problem to problem. For example, for many children, a drawing of a person may be more concrete than using a chip or block to represent a person, even though that chip or block is a concrete object that can be moved.

Kindergarten teachers must think about ways to offer children a broad spectrum of concrete materials. For example, early in the year, problems about items that are available in the classroom (crayons, pencils, cups, books, and people) allow the children to model the problem with real objects. When problems refer to a wider range of items, felt-constructed models can meet the needs of learners that still prefer real objects. Teddy bear counters can generally stand for other animals and for people as well. Over time, some children are equally comfortable with chips or blocks that can represent any object. Yet at this age you'll see that many children often choose a manipulative material that is related to the object under consideration. For example, orange Cuisenaire rods will be chosen to model a story about carrots.

During the kindergarten-through-second-grade years, several changes take place. Children learn to reliably count quantities and to recognize the number in a small set of objects without counting. They develop more sophisticated counting strategies such as counting on, counting back, and skip counting. They develop strategies based on number relationships that allow them to find sums and differences without counting. They become able to retrieve basic addition and subtraction facts. The range of numbers with which the children can work broadens.

Such growth of understanding results from many experiences with counting and solving problems. It comes from sharing ideas and listening to others. It comes from teachers who know when to probe deeper and when to stay silent. It does not, however, always follow a straight and predictable path. Some kindergarten children can accomplish tasks that second graders find very difficult. Children who can do something today may falter tomorrow as they move in and out of their conceptual understandings. It is important, therefore, for teachers at these grade levels to recognize a broad spectrum of number problems and skills. Let's consider problem solving in a kindergarten classroom.

The Enormous Watermelon

In early May, a kindergarten class is exploring a unit on growing things. Since they have just planted seeds, the teacher introduces a book titled *The Enormous Watermelon*, by Brenda Parkes, Judith Smith, and Mary Davy. The text is appropriate for emergent readers, as it is highly predictable. The characters—Old Mother Hubbard, Humpty Dumpty, Wee Willie Winky, Jack and Jill, and Little Miss Muffet—are familiar to the children. The class began the year with a focus on nursery rhymes. Within this familiar literary genre, the children explored activities related to prediction, rhyme, and repetitive language.

In this story, Old Mother Hubbard plants some watermelon seeds and eventually goes out to her garden to pick a watermelon. It is so big, however, that she must ask for help. One at a time, a character is introduced who comes to help Old Mother Hubbard pull the watermelon home. Finally, when there are six people, they are able to pull the watermelon to Old Mother Hubbard's home.

On the first day the story is read, the emphasis is placed on predicting the next character that will come to help. (Illustrations associated with each character, such as a wall, a spider, and an overturned pail are shown on the page before the corresponding new character is introduced.) The children are excited when they recognize the authors' technique of introducing characters and they are proud of their ability to make predictions. When the children see the candlestick, they are certain that Jack is coming next to nimbly jump the candlestick. They are surprised when it is Wee Willie Winky who carries the candlestick as he runs through the town. The teacher believes that the authors and illustrator have purposely created this false expectation, to remind children that the words are also important in a story and that not all predictions are correct, even if they make sense.

On the second day the story is read, the emphasis is on the word *enormous*, and the size of the watermelon is further connected to the number of people needed to pull it home. On the third day, the children act out the story. Name tags with the characters' names are given to six of the children to dramatize the story as it is read. This is repeated until each child has the opportunity to take an active role in the story.

It is after the children have achieved a high level of familiarity with the story that a mathematical problem is posed: *How many hands did it take to pull the watermelon home?* The teacher has recorded the problem on a large piece of chart paper. She reads it to them and then they reread it a couple of times together. Once she is certain that the children understand what is written, she gives each of them a copy of the problem on a piece of paper that provides room for them to record their work.

The children are familiar with receiving problems in this format. They have been using "recording sheets" since the fall. Over the course of the year, the children have become much more adept at recording both their answers and how they arrived at those answers. These representations serve several purposes. At this young age, recording helps the children remember what they did, and thus makes it easier for them to share their thinking with others. Children come to see that how they think about a problem is as important as the answers they get. Also, the mere act of representing their thinking can be a transformative experience. Over time, recordings can help implicit, informal ideas to become explicit and formalized. The sharing of these different representations helps children to realize that a variety of responses and ways of thinking are possible. Eventually, it helps children to link different representations of the same idea.

For this problem, almost all of the children draw six people or six sets of hands and then count the hands. Yet within this common approach, there is great variation. Madison draws a pair of hands and then makes a line to the right. "That's one person and two hands," she announces. She draws a second set of hands and says, "That's another person and two more hands. Now I have two people." She continues verbalizing her thinking and recounting the pairs as she draws each set of hands (see Figure 3–1). Once she has six sets of hands, she counts the hands and records the twelve.

Duncan also draws six people and, like Madison, he recounts his figures after he completes each one. He then begins

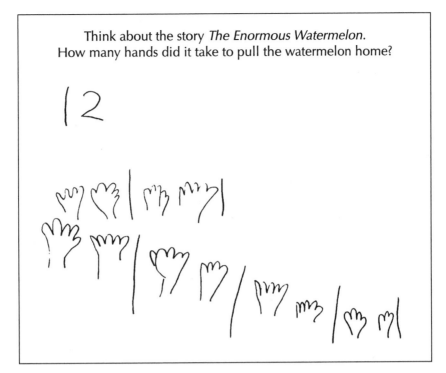

> Think about the story *The Enormous Watermelon*.
> How many hands did it take to pull the watermelon home?
>
> 12

FIGURE 3–1   *Madison's work*

to count each hand and looses his place. He turns to the Jackie, who is sitting next to him and says, "Uh-oh, I think I already counted that one. I better write this down." Jackie replies in a supportive manner: "That's OK. I do that too." After recording the number of each hand, Duncan also writes the answer—12— at the top of his sheet (see Figure 3–2). Duncan's teacher notes that he has reversed his 3, 7, and 9, but is pleased that his other numbers are written correctly.

Renee's response is similar, but her work places the figures in context. She enjoys illustrating the story (see Figure 3–3), drawing a line of figures engaged in pulling the watermelon home. When there is no more room on the page, Renee counts the figures in her drawing. "Yikes," she exclaims, "I have nine and I only need six." She then crosses out the last three figures and counts, tapping her pencil on each side of the remaining people. She finally records 12 as her answer.

FIGURE 3–2   *Duncan's work*

Morgan is also involved with representing the story. He varies the way his characters look and includes the watermelon in his drawing (see Figure 3–4 on page 44). He even tries to record the names of the characters: Humpty Dumpty, Old Mother Hubbard, Jack, Jill, and Wee Willy Winky. The fact that there are six people is compelling to him, but he does not note the two-to-one relationship between people and hands. Morgan certainly knows that people have two hands, but the notion of a two-to-one correspondence that can be applied generally is an underdeveloped idea. Morgan shows his recording to his teacher and they have the following conversation.

MORGAN: Here's mine.

TEACHER: I SEE YOU DREW THE CHARACTERS AND WROTE THEIR NAMES AS WELL.

Think about the story *The Enormous Watermelon.*
How many hands did it take to pull the watermelon home?

12

FIGURE 3–3   *Renee's work*

MORGAN: Yep, all six are here.

TEACHER: IS THAT WHAT THESE SIXES MEAN? *[She points to the numerals on his drawing.]*

MORGAN: This six is for the number of people and this six is for the number of hands.

TEACHER: CAN I WRITE THAT? *[Morgan nods and the teacher labels the two numbers so that it is clear what they represent. She has found that when she keeps work, she sometimes forgets its meaning. She has learned to make notes in order to jog her memory.]*

TELL ME, COULD THERE BE ONLY SIX HANDS FOR SIX PEOPLE?

MORGAN: No, that would be silly. *[He giggles.]*

TEACHER: HOW MANY WOULD THERE BE?

MORGAN: More.

TEACHER: DO YOU KNOW HOW MANY MORE?

MORGAN: More than six.

Think about the story *The Enormous Watermelon.*
How many hands did it take to pull the watermelon home?

6 (people)
6 (hands)

oDmTHerhBD
wewlewke
TAK
HteDPS
TILL

FIGURE 3–4   *Morgan's work*

Manny also draws six people (see Figure 3–5). When he counts to find the number of hands, he first counts all of the arms he drew on the left side of the figures, then the arms he drew on the right side of the figures. He records 6 + 6 = 12, brings his representation to his teacher, and has this brief conversation.

TEACHER: HOW DID YOU FIND YOUR ANSWER?
  MANNY: I drew six people and counted their arms.
TEACHER: TELL ME ABOUT WHAT YOU WROTE HERE *[pointing to the equation]*.
  MANNY: Here's the arms I counted *[pointing to the two 6s]* and six and six are twelve.
TEACHER: DID YOU COUNT TO FIND THE TWELVE?
  MANNY: No, I just knew it.

Manny's teacher marvels at the variation in one child's thinking. A few years ago, before she placed so much emphasis

Think about the story *The Enormous Watermelon*.
How many hands did it take to pull the watermelon home?

$$6 + 6 = 12$$

FIGURE 3–5   *Manny's work*

on children showing and telling what they knew, she never would have guessed that a child who had memorized that six plus six is twelve would need to count the six hands on the right after determining that there were six hands on the left. She has learned that for some children, a recognizable fact is simple, while what she might recognize as a simple one-to-one relationship is more abstract.

Lizzy counts aloud by twos, placing down a finger each time she says a number. When she has six fingers placed down, she says, "That's it, twelve," and records 12 on her paper. Then she draws pairs of hands, and records the numbers she said when she counted by twos (see Figure 3–6, page 46). She looks at her drawing a bit and then decides to count the number of hands in one column. Upon noting the six, she then records 6 + 6 = to the left of her answer so that an equation is formed.

Gerald illustrates the situation, but only partially (see Figure 3–7, page 47). He then records the equation 2 + 2 = 4. To the right of this equation, he records 4 + 4 = 8. He then writes two more equations, adding two to eight and then two to ten. He brings his paper to his teacher and announces that the answer is 12. When the ubiquitous question, "How do you know?" is asked, he responds, "I found two people, doubled that, and then added the last two on."

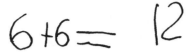

Think about the story *The Enormous Watermelon.*
How many hands did it take to pull the watermelon home?

FIGURE 3–6   *Lizzy's work*

Teacher Reflection

When I first began teaching, I would have told Morgan why six hands was the incorrect answer. I might have involved Morgan in the process, such as having six children line up so that he could count their hands, but it still would have been me giving him access to the answer. Now, I rely more on the children and follow their lead.

If Morgan had seemed interested in knowing the exact number, I would have asked him what we could do to find the answer. But Morgan was satisfied with

Think about the story *The Enormous Watermelon*.
How many hands did it take to pull the watermelon home?

$$8 + 2 = 10$$

$$10 + 2 = 21$$

$$2 + 2 = 4$$

$$4 + 4 = 8$$

FIGURE 3–7 *Gerald's work*

the fact that there were more than six. He loves litera-
ture and writing and I didn't want to detract from his
enjoyment of this story. "More than six" is enough for
today. Later I will spend some time with him exploring
activities that support the development of two-to-one
relationships. I also believe that when we share solutions and strategies together as a class, he will benefit
from hearing his peers' answers.

I should learn not to be surprised by the range of
responses my students make to a problem such as *The
Enormous Watermelon*, but I always am. I want problems
like this one to challenge my students as they continue
to develop proficiency and accuracy in counting. I

believe that such tasks will lead children to ideas about addition and other operations. Sometimes I increase the challenge of such problems by making the total number greater; other times I do it by making the problems more complex. In this problem the children need to keep track of both the number of people and the number of hands. I know this is not easy. Morgan reminds me of the difficulties many young children have.

Originally, I wasn't quite able to follow Gerald's response. I was thrilled by his use of equations, but when he said, "I found two people, doubled that, and then added the last two on," I was taken a back. How was Gerald making sense of this? How does what he said relate to his written response? Is he able to show me where the six people or six hands are represented in his equations? As he spoke, I knew I wasn't completely following his thinking, but his confidence and correct answer, along with the few students waiting for my assistance, made me move on.

Later, when I had a little time, I realized what his work showed. His original equation, $2 + 2 = 4$, stands for the hands on two different people. When he doubles this, he establishes eight hands. By adding two to the eight and then two to the ten, he accounts for two more sets of hands, for a total of twelve hands. He reverses the digits in his final recording, but I know he recognizes that the answer is twelve.

Keeping track of what is counted is a complex issue. It requires children to think about their work, to be cognitively aware of their thinking processes as they complete a task. I never would have kept track of the number of hands and people in the way that Gerald did. Gerald's work has opened new possibilities to me.

This teacher reminds us of the wide variety in children's thinking. She also shows us how deeply a reflective teacher thinks about her students' work and how to best challenge their thinking. Even though an older child or adult would solve this problem simply by using multiplication, for kindergarten children, it provides a counting challenge. It may lead some children to implement counting-on strategies or addition. It also exposes children to the repeated counting of equal groups, planting a seed for future ideas.

Ants on the Ground

In general, the problems given to first-grade students don't necessarily differ a great deal from those given to kindergarten students. The numbers can be greater, it doesn't take so long to set up a context for a problem, and many children are beginning to read the problems on their own. The problems at both levels, however, tend to focus on basic joining and separating actions that require children to determine the unknown total or the unknown part that is left. What is different is the way older children think about these problems and the way they can represent that thinking.

The following problem was given to first-grade students in late January.

> There are 12 ants on the ground.
> Then 4 ants go down their ant hole.
> How many ants are still on the ground?

As in kindergarten, many children use manipulative materials to solve the problem. In her representation (Figure 3–8), Maki used bears for the ants, because she's working with teddy bear counters. She uses arrows to depict the four ants that separate from the group. She then uses arrows in another symbolic representation of this separation. This representation shows that she can think of each subset as a distinct group that doesn't have to be shown as a group of ones.

Rocco uses beans. He writes, rather than draws, to tell what he did (see Figure 3–9). He reads his explanation aloud to his teacher: "I pulled four away and I looked at the other pile and I counted. The other pile had to be eight." Miranda also uses beans. She rings a group of four without noticeably counting them, then she records a subtraction equation (see Figure 3–10).

I uesd 12bears.

4 ← → 8

FIGURE 3–8   *Maki's work*

I Puld 4 uWa and
I luKt at the uthre
Piul and I Koutib
the uther Pieul hadtbe
8

FIGURE 3–9   *Rocco's work*

Hands are often a point of reference. With numbers greater than ten, however, other objects must be used. Carmine uses a block and a pencil to model the two additional ants. He pushes the block and pencil away as he folds under two of his fingers. The three-part sequence in his representation (Figure 3–11, page 52) will easily translate into a number sentence when he is ready.

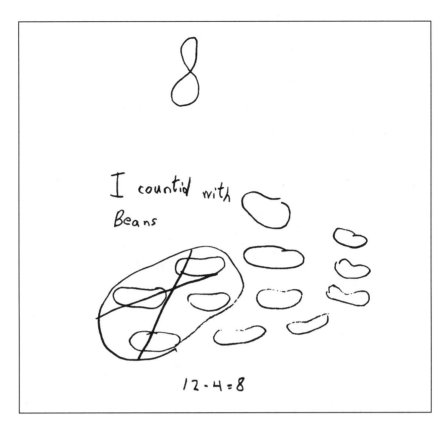

FIGURE 3–10   *Miranda's work*

Janel uses hands as well, merely adding two fingers after she traces her own hands. She writes the equation 10 + 2 = 12 to show how she formed her initial set. Rather than a take-away strategy, Janel counts back saying, "twelve, eleven, ten, nine, eight," as she touches four of the fingers. She records her answer, 8, and then looks at her drawing a bit. She identifies a group of four fingers by labeling them with the numbers 1 through 4 (Figure 3–12, page 53).

These representations illustrate some of the subtle differences that occur during first grade. The children write more. They tend to emphasize the sequential action of a story. Some incorporate more than one representation. They develop new counting strategies and suggest set recognition.

These basic problem structures continue to be considered in second grade, but the numbers get bigger. In fact, these same problems can be found in the upper elementary grades incorporating

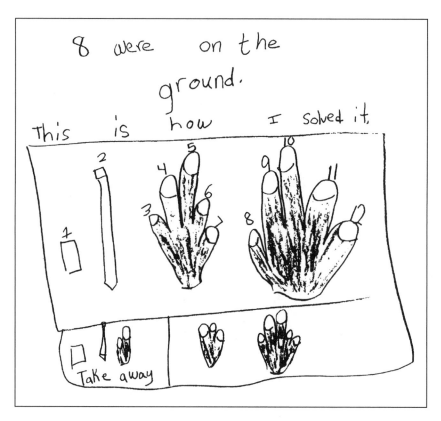

FIGURE 3–11   *Carmine's work*

decimals and fractions. Yet there are ways other than changing the numbers to increase the difficulty level of addition and subtraction problems.

Looking at Addition and Subtraction Problems

There are different types of addition and subtraction problems involving joining, separating, comparing, and looking at the relations of parts to whole. Consider this basic joining problem:

>Millie has 7 stamps from France.
>Her grandmother gives her 6 stamps from Egypt.
>How many stamps does Millie have now?

The problem is fairly simple and would be appropriate for children in kindergarten or first grade. The action in the problem is

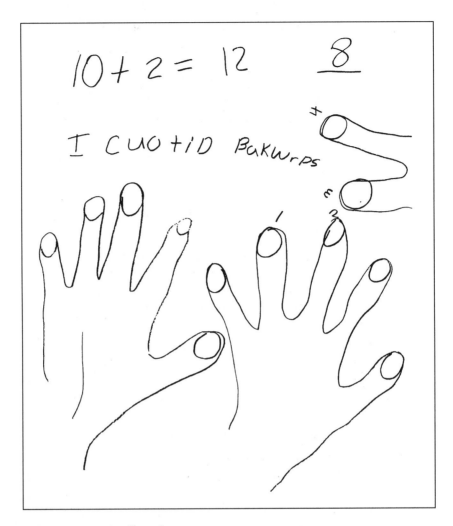

FIGURE 3–12   *Janel's work*

clear and the information is given in the order in which it can be used.

In second grade, students may be given the same problem, but with two- or three-digit numbers. Due to the basic format of the problem, students can simply operate mechanically on the numbers. This is reasonable when children are exploring ways to add large numbers. The focus is on the addition itself; the challenge is to find the correct sum rather than to analyze the meaning of the problem.

From a problem-solving perspective, however, it is important that students continue to explore story problems that must be considered carefully in order to interpret the situation correctly. Return to the joining problem introduced earlier. The difficulty increases if one of the parts, rather than the total, is unknown. For example, consider the problems below.

> Millie's mom gave her some stamps from France.
> Then her grandmother gave her 6 stamps from Egypt.
> Now Millie has 13 stamps.
> How many stamps did Millie get from her mom?

> Millie's mom gave her 7 stamps from France.
> Then her grandma gave her some stamps from Egypt.
> Now Millie has 13 stamps.
> How many stamps did Millie get from her grandma?

A teacher gave the second problem above to her second-grade class in late October. Jimmy, who solves a traditional joining problem by adding seven and six, begins by making seven tally marks to represent the stamps from France. Then he continues to make tally marks while counting on to thirteen. But since he did not separate his groups (an unnecessary step when looking for the unknown total), he does not know his answer. He crosses this work out and begins again. This time he makes tally marks for the stamps from France, but uses circles for the stamps from Egypt. He then counts to find the number of circles he made. He counts the circles by twos (see Figure 3–13).

Bethany uses her fingers to find the answer. She starts at seven and counts on to thirteen, putting out a finger for each number she says. In this way she is using her fingers not to denote the second set per se, but to keep track of her count.

Over time, children begin to recognize that the relationship between 7, 6, and 13 remains constant, regardless of which of the numbers is missing. Even these children, however, may initially have difficulty recognizing the answer. Note Marie's work (Figure 3–14) and Joe's work (Figure 3–15). Both students are able to relate this problem to the basic fact, but are unable to identify the correct answer.

6 ,4 ,2
6

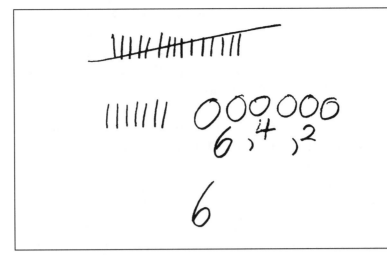

FIGURE 3–13 *Jimmy's work*

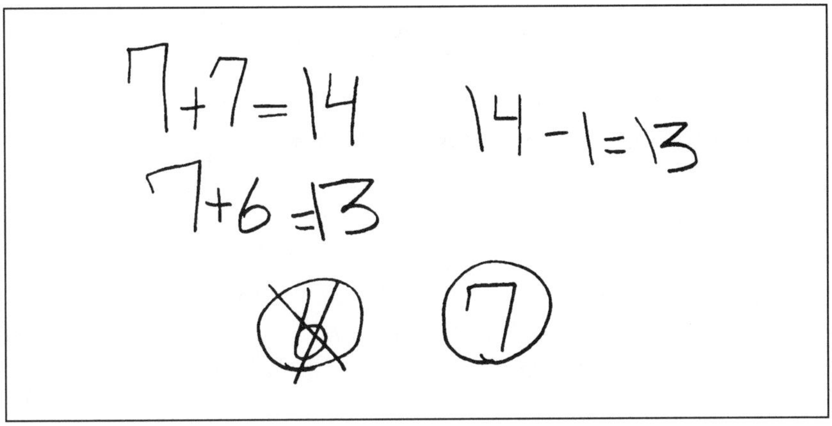

7+7=14
14-1=13
7+6=13
7

FIGURE 3–14 *Marie's work*

I know first she had 7
and 7+6=13 so thirteen
is the answer.

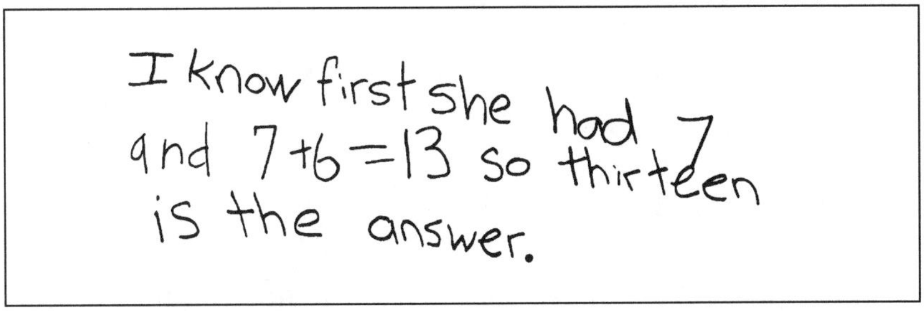

FIGURE 3–15 *Joe's work*

Separating problems can also be written with any one of the three numbers missing. Both joining and separating problems involve an action. When the final number is missing, the problem is easier to solve, as the information is given in the order it can be modeled. The most difficult problems are those that omit the initial number, as children aren't sure how to begin.

Two other problem structures are possible. Comparison problems are often introduced after separating problems. Consider the problems below.

Norm has 8 blocks.
Brenda has 15 blocks.
How many more blocks does Brenda have than Norm?

Norm has 8 blocks.
Brenda has 7 more blocks than Norm.
How many blocks does Brenda have?

Norm has some blocks.
Brenda has 7 more blocks than Norm.
Brenda has 15 blocks.
How many blocks does Norm have?

Note that these problems involve a comparative relationship, rather than an action. Finally, there are part-whole problems that do not involve a comparison or an action.

Jason has 15 blocks.
Some are large and 7 are small.
How many of the blocks are large?

Jason has 15 blocks.
Eight blocks are blue.
The rest of the blocks are red.
How many blocks are red?

It is not necessary for teachers to memorize each of these (different) types of problems. Nor do children need to identify them. What is important is that teachers vary the formats of the problems they give to their students so that they provide challenge and a broader mathematical perspective.

A research program at the University of Wisconsin has studied how children solve these different types of problems. Once the researchers studied the way in which children thought about mathematics, they used this knowledge to help teachers think about their students' work. This Cognitively Guided Instruction (CGI) encourages teachers to focus on the intuitive ways children solve a variety of problems and the ways in which their skills develop over time. Teachers unfamiliar with this work are encouraged to read more about CGI and to explore the different problem structures in their classrooms (see Carpenter et al. 1999).

Teacher Reflection

Learning about different problem types has really opened my eyes and helped me look at my second grade students' work somewhat differently. I know it is important for them to really solidify basic addition and subtraction facts, but having them apply this skill to different, often more challenging problems, makes me wonder what it really means to "know their facts." I now see why it is so important to vary the numbers, the context, and the type of problems I ask my students to solve.

Having children show their representations to others, has helped to make problem solving strategies explicit. My students don't hide their fingers anymore when they decide to count all or count on. I'm glad that I have gotten rid of that old taboo in my classroom. I want to embrace the way my students make sense of mathematical situations. I am thrilled when children reach for manipulatives to help them in new situations and gratified when that realize that they no longer need them. It is seeing the children make sense of the ideas of addition and subtraction, rather than just operating rotely with the numbers, that is the most rewarding.

Developing Basic Facts

At the end of the second grade, students should be able to retrieve and utilize basic addition and subtraction facts. This doesn't mean that all facts must be memorized. Many adults find the answer to 9 + 7 by thinking of the equation 10 + 7 – 1. The difference in time it takes to find 16 this way rather than through automatic recall is insignificant.

Years ago, children were asked to memorize basic facts one table at a time. Once the two's table was memorized, the three's table was studied. These tables were not related to each other, nor was the two's table necessarily related to addition. The task was usually accompanied by timed tests. Children who were good at memorization were quite successful. But even these children had a limited understanding of the relationships among these numbers. Children who were not good at memorization often learned to dislike mathematics and believed it was not something they could do.

More recently, children have received instruction in basic fact strategies. Textbooks offer specific lessons on different strategies as new facts are introduced. For example, children might be taught that they can find 6 + 7 by thinking about 6 + 6 + 1. While an improvement over mere memorization, such directive teaching often leads to ideas, quickly forgotten, that really weren't understood in the first place. Or even if remembered, sometimes such ideas are not trusted as reliable. It is much more powerful to have children construct these strategies themselves. Through conversations, they can build on one another's ideas and choose to embrace a classmate's technique as their own. In this manner the mathematics is developed by the children, not delivered by the teacher. Thus, children learn that mathematics is something that they can do and comprehend. Many teachers who used to teach fact strategies directly are now rethinking this practice.

Teacher Reflection

When I first learned about fact strategies, I thought that they were the answer to my prayers. I introduced the children to strategies until they had enough tools to find all of the facts. It seemed such a better approach then making them just memorize the tables. I continued to use timed tests, but had the children focus on their improvement. Each child answered as many fact problems as possible in two minutes. Individual graphs were made showing how the children improved over time. In that way, the children were only competing against themselves. I followed this practice for a couple of years and felt good about what I was doing.

Then one day in early October, I was sitting in the kitchen with my granddaughter who was in the second grade. She was counting the cookies we had just decorated. There were four cookies on one plate and five on another. I asked her how many cookies we had decorated so far. She said five aloud and then counted six, seven, eight, nine as she placed a finger down for each number in order to know when she had said four numbers.

I decided this was a perfect opportunity to teach her about using doubles. I asked, "Could five plus five help you find the answer?" She looked a bit confused at first, but then she said, "Oh, I know what you mean. Five plus five is ten. Then five plus four is nine because it's one less." She obviously knew the strategy. I wondered why she didn't use it and asked her about it. "Well, that's my teacher's way, but I like to count."

I was really taken back by her reply. It made me think about my second-grade students and whether or not they were just mimicking what I had told them. Over time, I changed what I did. I gave more emphasis to story problems and to dice games that required students to find sums and differences. I let their ideas lead the way. I let them use their techniques, rather than mine.

Through exposure to problems with small numbers, young children begin to know that 2 + 2 = 4 and that 3 + 3 = 6. They also easily learn that 5 + 5 = 10. When asked, most claim to *just know* these facts. Visual images can help other doubles to be learned. The arrangement of dots on dominoes can be helpful here. Dominoes can also provide children with visual images of other combinations. Such images help children learn the facts in a way that makes sense to them.

Some classrooms use ten-frames to help children become familiar with number relationships. Ten frames are two-by-five grids in which dots or counters can be placed to represent numbers. They help children to recognize quantity and establish numerical relationships. A ten-frame with eight counters on it (Figure 3–16) is a visual representation which enables children to "see" that eight is two less than ten and three more than five. Being able to group numbers in different ways helps children to derive facts. For example, to find 8 + 5, a child might think of taking 2 from the 5 to complete the ten-frame, leaving 3, for an answer of 13. Or, he or she might think about adding the 5 from the top row of the ten-frame to the other 5, getting 10. Then the remaining 3 is added to get 13.

Dice games can give students opportunities to think about and share addition and subtraction strategies. These strategies include counting techniques, relating combinations to known facts, and decomposing numbers to combine them in different ways. There are numerous games, both commercially made and available in curriculum materials, that are easily utilized in primary classrooms. While six-sided dice are the norm in kindergarten classrooms, some first- and second-grade classrooms also use dice with a greater number of faces. These dice allow for a greater variety of numbers to be used. As children play a dice game, they often naturally verbalize their thinking.

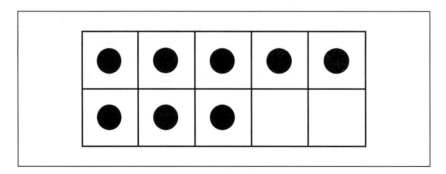

FIGURE 3–16   *Ten-frame with eight counters*

In early December first-grade students are playing with one traditional dice cube and a polyhedron die labeled with the numbers 0 through 9. In pairs, the children take turns rolling the dice and seeing if they can agree on the total number. Jessica and Kiwa are working together. Jessica rolls first. She rolls a 5 and a 0. She and her partner, Kiwa, easily recognize the sum.

JESSICA: That's easy. It's five. Five and nothing is five.
KIWA: I agree. That's so easy. Anything with zero is easy.

Kiwa rolls next. She rolls a 9 and a 6. She extends her fingers and begins to mumble to herself the numbers one through nine. Each time she says a new number, she touches a new finger to her chin. When she gets to nine, she holds out her nine extended fingers. "Nine," she repeats to herself. Then Kiwa again touches her fingers to her chin, one at a time, as she says the numbers one through six. She extends the five tapped fingers on one hand and the one finger on the other hand and looks at them for a bit. Next she reforms her hand to show nine extended fingers and announces the number, nine, loudly. She leaves her fingers in this formation and says, "ten, eleven, twelve, thirteen, fourteen, fifteen," while tapping one of the fingers she had used to show the six, each time she says a number. When her teacher asked how she knew when to stop counting, Kiwa explained, "I can see the six fingers."

While Kiwa was using her fingers, Jessica counted on from nine while pointing to the six dots on the die. They agreed the answer was fifteen. Her teacher asked Jessica if she could have counted from the six as well. "You could, but then I wouldn't have the nine dots." (This die shows numerals rather than dots.) "Also," she continued, "it's better to start with the big one. You don't have to count so much."

At first, young children find sums by counting each set separately and then counting the two groups after they are combined. Counting on, versus counting all, is a more sophisticated strategy. Recognizing that you can count on from either number comes later. This is an important mathematical idea. It requires the child to recognize that the sum will be the same regardless of the order of the addends.

Brendan and Eric are playing the same game. Brendan rolls a 5 and a 4. He quickly shows five fingers on one hand and four fingers on the other. He looks briefly at the configuration of his fingers and says, "Five and four is nine." His teacher asked how he knew the answer so quickly. "Cause I almost used every finger," he replied. "Every finger is ten."

After the children have had the opportunity to play the game a few times, the teacher brings his students together to talk about their strategies. He tells the children, "Imagine that you are playing the dice game and roll a six and a four. How could you find the total?"

FRANK: I count four more: seven, eight, nine, ten.

DONNA: I know six, so four more is ten because it uses up all your fingers. *[Donna holds up six fingers and then extends the remaining four to show ten. She didn't need to count; she has a visual image for this combination.]*

PAUL: With four and six, you take one from the six and put it on the four. Then you have five and five to make ten.

ALYSSA: I can take the four apart and get two and two. Then I can go two, four, six to make six. *[As she says these last three numbers, she holds up one finger for each number she says.]* Then I can go eight, ten. *[These numbers are said as she extends two more fingers.]* Four and six is ten.

Teacher Reflection

I think it is very important to give my first graders a lot of opportunities to work with "basic facts." I want them to work with single-digit addends in a variety of ways, even though they won't recognize it as fact work. I know that at the beginning of the year, the students usually count to add two numbers. I know it can take a long time for children to move beyond this stage, but I don't think time is the only factor.

I believe that children need to explore adding. By playing a myriad of games, I see that over time, the children move from counting every item, to counting on. This is an important step for first graders.

I really like the variety in their thinking. While one child is still counting on, another is using fact strategies. I try to acknowledge and honor the different ways of thinking. I want children to see mathematics as a process of making sense, not just of finding a right answer.

More and more children are involved with making sense of addition and subtraction as they show and tell their ideas. As we'll see in the next chapter, this process is not limited to work with basic facts. It can be extended to larger numbers as well.

4

Representing Numbers and Operations

Have you ever counted pennies in order to identify a collection of fifty to place in a roll? Did you ever lose track of your count and have to ask yourself, "Did I count that one already?" or "Am I at thirty or forty?" Many people have this experience. The frustration of having to recount leads some of us to make the conscious decision to group the pennies, perhaps by fives or tens. If the count is lost again, the grouping helps us to reestablish the total more quickly.

Our number system is organized in groups of ten. It is a highly efficient system, as it allows us to write all numbers with just the ten digits 0 through 9. This way of counting is a marvelous invention. We have a number system that is simple and elegant, yet embodies many complex ideas. Between entering kindergarten and completing the second grade, students are expected to gain a solid understanding of these concepts. As we listen to children and look at their representations, we can learn much about this process. We also need to think about the numerical language and models we present to children.

Miles, a kindergarten student, is counting aloud. He reaches twenty and says the number names twenty-one through twenty-eight quickly. He then says twenty-nine in a drawn-out manner while he tries to recall the next number. He says twenty-nine again and a classmate whispers, "thirty." Miles then counts quickly and with confidence until thirty-nine is reached. He draws out the number, thirty-nine, until his classmate helps again by whispering, "forty." Miles's counting then proceeds quickly until he reaches forty-nine.

The rhythm of his counting suggests that Miles has discovered a pattern in our number system. He recognizes that once he identifies a new decade, such as forty, he can then repeat the cycle one through nine. Deciding what number comes after a number such as forty-nine is difficult for him. Emerging counters tend to focus on the ones digits and are less aware of the pattern within the tens digits. They don't formally recognize that once they reach nine in the ones place, the tens digit must change. They maintain their focus on the ones place, rather than thinking about what comes after the forties. As a result, many suggest forty-ten for the next number. It takes quite a while for children to recognize the multiple cycles of zero through nine within our way of counting.

One of the simple, yet powerful ideas of our number system is that a ten represents both ten units and one ten. Return to our pennies for a moment and imagine three piles of ten pennies and four scattered pennies. How would you count the pennies? Most of us would probably think ten, twenty, thirty, thirty-one, thirty-two, thirty-three, thirty-four. Yet, we could also think one, two, three tens, and one, two, three, four ones—thirty-four. Ideally, we are able to think in both ways, depending on the situation. But how does one gain this flexible thinking and a deep understanding of these nested loops of numbers? How do children understand numbers in relationship to one another? How do the representational models within our classrooms affect learning outcomes?

How Many Days Have We Been in School?

Including the question "How many days have we been in school?" within morning routines is a common practice in many primary classrooms. Since there are approximately 180 days of school each year, this activity offers young children opportunities to think about and work with larger numbers. They gain exposure to patterns within our number system as well as build their number sense.

Some teachers use a number line, hung around the classroom, as a model for keeping track of the number of days in school. As the numbers increase, the length of the line increases as well. The number line is a powerful tool and having one situated in the classroom for reference is valuable. It gives children a visual image of how far twenty-five is from zero, whether forty-two comes before or after thirty-seven, and the difference between sixty-nine and seventy-one. It also presents a continuous model of our number system, one to which decimals, fractions, and negative numbers can someday be included, as well as the notion of infinity.

Other teachers feel that the number line is too cumbersome for young children and choose to use a blank 18-by-10 grid. As each day passes, the number is recorded on the chart. Because the numbers are written in rows of ten, students may more readily see number patterns emerge. Conversations such as the one in this kindergarten classroom are commonplace.

TEACHER: WHERE SHOULD WE PRINT THE NUMBER FOR TODAY?
    JESS: I think it goes under the fifty-one. Today is sixty-one.
    MAX: We already used six whole rows, so we need to start another one.
    DAVE: After sixty is sixty-one, so you go to the next box. There isn't a box next to sixty, so you have to move down.
    ANGIE: If you went down one box that would be seventy. You have to go under the fifty-one, like Jess said.

These students are making sense of how to use the grid, and their comments reflect their growing ideas about our number system. Kindergarten, first-, and second-grade students can all benefit from such work. While older children may begin to see patterns based on multiples, younger children see patterns within the tens and ones emerge as the chart fills up one day at a time. The left-to-right progression follows what they are learning in terms of directionality when reading and writing, including the return sweep to a new row or line.

In first or second grade, some teachers choose to highlight the odd and even numbers by recording with alternating red and blue markers. Some teachers use highlighting tape to accentuate a specific column or row. Such techniques lead to new discoveries, as captured in this first-grade conversation.

GRETCHEN: I noticed that all of the fives go down—five, fifteen, twenty-five, thirty-five, forty-five, fifty-five, sixty-five [*while pointing to the 5 on the chart and drawing her finger down the column*].

LISA: They all have five on one side. Fifty-five has two fives.

MARVIN: I see that. I can do that with eight, too: eight, eighteen, twenty-eight, thirty-eight, forty-eight, fifty-eight, sixty-eight. There isn't one yet with two eights.

TEACHER: DO YOU THINK WE MIGHT COME TO ONE WITH TWO EIGHTS?

WILL: Yes, eighty-eight. It will go under sixty-eight, then seventy-eight, then eighty-eight.

On another day the children focus on the pattern that emerges when they consider the tens column. Though they do not talk in terms of tens and ones when working with the chart, they begin to see the cyclical way we use the digits 0–9 when writing numbers. The interplay between the columns and rows is both geometrically interesting and numerically significant. One child expresses an idea about the top row of numbers. She suggests, "I think these numbers are like a guide. They go one, two, three, four, five, six, seven, eight, nine, ten. We follow that pattern all the way."

The idea of getting to one hundred can be highly motivating to kindergarten students. They seem to have a sense of one hundred as being a big number and they are excited by the prospect of having spent one hundred days in school. The importance some children give to this number is illustrated by one child's query: "Is this when we go to first grade?"

The teacher decides to build on their interest by asking, "Where do you think we will write the number one hundred on our chart?" Many children think that it will be recorded in the bottom right-hand corner of the 18-by-10 grid. It is almost as if one hundred is the last number for them. As the number of days increases, some children are willing to make a different prediction. They are clearly intrigued with the idea that you could count from one to one hundred and identify a square that is not the last one on the chart. A few children begin to count by tens down the right column and concur with the students who count by ones.

The teacher is interested in the conversations her original question has provoked. She is impressed with what some of her students can do and unsure about what some of the others are understanding. On the seventy-third day of school, after many days of brief discussions at meeting time, she decides to give each child his or her own small copy of the chart. She wants to learn how her students decide where to mark 100 on the grid when they work independently. She wants to determine who is making sense of the whole-group discussions. Due to her high interest level, she sets aside time to have each child mark his or her own chart in her presence.

As expected, quite a few children automatically write 100 in the last square. Several other students begin by reading the numbers from one to seventy-three and then continue their count to one hundred. Most of these children identify the correct location. Marcus records a 1 and four 0s in that position (see Figure 4–1). He explains, "One hundred is a very big number. It's hard to write it in the box."

Some students miscount by one or two. Frank originally lands on the square for 102. He explains, "This is one hundred, but it doesn't seem right. I think the zeros go over here." He points to the right end of that row. He marks 100 in the spot where 110 would go. While he did not identify the correct location, he correctly recognizes 100 as belonging in the same column as the other numbers ending in zero.

Anita, Laurie, and Terrance count on from seventy-three. They all write 100 in the correct square. A small group of children count by tens, starting at ten, and do so successfully. Rosemary says, "Ten, twenty, thirty, forty, fifty, sixty, seventy, eighty, ninety, one hundred! It helps to count by tens. I know it goes here." She then prints 100 in the correct location.

As of today, our Number of Days in School chart looks like this.

We have been wondering, "Are we going to get to 100?" Where might you write 100 to show the one-hundredth day of school?

1	2	3	4	5	6	7	8	9	10
11	12	13	14	15	16	17	18	19	20
21	22	23	24	25	26	27	28	29	30
31	32	33	34	35	36	37	38	39	40
41	42	43	44	45	46	47	48	49	50
51	52	53	54	55	56	57	58	59	60
61	62	63	64	65	66	67	68	69	70
71	72	73							
									10000

FIGURE 4–1 *Marcus's recording of 100*

Teacher Reflection

Though clearly many children still think of one hundred as the last number on the chart, I was impressed with how well some of them negotiated this task. It is still early in the year and already they are beginning to see patterns within our number system. It is important that even young children have opportunities to make predictions based on patterns they observe. I know that as the days increase, more of them will identify the correct placement. It will be exciting to watch them gain confidence in their conjectures.

Class discussions that offer children opportunities to explore our number system are powerful and impressive. For some children, this is all they need to move forward with their own thinking. For others, the dynamics of a large group are overwhelming and often give some permission to tune out. Making sure to balance these large-group conversations with small-group or individual work is critical to me. I really want to have access to each child's thinking. Sometimes, that means I must figure out a way to talk with students individually about their work, even if only for a few moments.

The hundreds chart is similar in organization to the 18-by-10 grid. Commercially made boards with removable number tiles are easily obtained and are attractive to students. Lisa is in the first grade and refers to the hundreds board as her "number puzzle." She likes to empty all the tiles on the table and then pick up a tile randomly, read the number, and decide where to place it on the board. Though she will accept help from a classmate, she likes doing this work independently.

For Xander, this same task is too cumbersome. He prefers to work with a partner and often needs help to read the numbers. You might hear him ask, "Is this forty-one or fourteen?" Xander seems to recognize when to ask for support; he knows that he often confuses the teen numbers. He has less difficulty when comparing eighty-five and fifty-eight. He knows eighty-five is "bigger" and thus, where to begin looking on the board. Given that the names of the teen numbers do not follow the same pattern as our other numbers, they often confuse students.

Other children find using the entire board a bit overwhelming. They prefer to take a handful of tiles and try to put them in order from least to greatest. By limiting how many tiles are available at a time, these children are more apt to be successful, and yet still gain a sense of working with the board. In a few cases, the teacher makes a smaller board, one that ends at forty. Note that it is important to continue to forty, rather than ending at thirty, so that students are exposed to two decades of numbers whose names begin with the tens place.

Tish and Richie develop their own game. They begin by filling the board together. Once convinced that they have all the tiles in the right place, one hides his or her eyes while the other removes a few blocks. When the child that removes the blocks says "Ready," the other child has to figure out which blocks are missing. These first-grade students work together well and their game is both appealing and mathematically challenging.

Tish hides her eyes first. Richie takes out the numbers 36, 45, 19, 88, 54 and 3 (see Figure 4–2). He reports, "Ready."

Tish uncovers her eyes. Pointing to the space between the 2 and the 4, she says, "That's easy; that's three." Richie checks the blocks in his hand and replaces the 3 in the empty spot.

Tish then asks, "Do you have nineteen?" Richie concurs. Next Tish puts her finger on 78, looks down and asks if 88 is missing. Richie again agrees.

It is interesting to note that Tish leaves the three empty spaces on the diagonal (36, 45, and 54) for last. Perhaps these were more challenging for her. To begin, she puts her finger on 26 and says, "Oh, it must be thirty-six, forty-six, fifty-six."

Richie responds, "Nope. Try again."

"It has to be thirty-six," protests Tish. "That's ten more."

Tish appears to want help. Richie replies, "Yup, it's thirty-six but . . ."

"Oh, I see. It goes back one," asserts Tish. She then identifies the missing 36 on the board correctly, places her finger on the 35, moves it to the space below, and says, "Forty-five."

Richie beams and responds, "Right again!" Tish then correctly identifies the missing 54.

1	2		4	5	6	7	8	9	10
11	12	13	14	15	16	17	18		20
21	22	23	24	25	26	27	28	29	30
31	32	33	34	35		37	38	39	40
41	42	43	44		46	47	48	49	50
51	52	53		55	56	57	58	59	60
61	62	63	64	65	66	67	68	69	70
71	72	73	74	75	76	77	78	79	80
81	82	83	84	85	86	87		89	90
91	92	93	94	95	96	97	98	99	100

FIGURE 4–2   *Game board with tiles removed*

For many first graders, work with a hundreds board is their first exposure to larger numbers. Thinking about this board as a puzzle is a good analogy. It is a puzzle to figure out how our number system works, how numbers are ordered, and how we write and say numbers. Some teachers help their students create hundreds boards by cutting up number lines and taping the groups of ten numbers together. Others cut up a hundreds chart to make a number line. In these ways, the two models of our number system can be connected.

While prepared charts or boards offer many important learning opportunities, it is important that children create their own representations. In one first-grade classroom, blank charts or grids are available for children to practice writing numbers.

Emily takes grid paper and writes numbers from 1 to 100. She begins by going across the top row from 1 to 10. When she comes to the spot for 11, she continues down the column, writing 11, 21, 31, 41, 51, 61, 71, 81, 91. She then returns to writing 12 next to 11 and continues 22, 32, 42, and so on. She works in this manner until she has all the spaces filled.

On a second sheet of grid paper she shades in one hundred squares (see Figures 4–3 and 4–4). "I wanted to see if it used the same," she explains.

"What do you mean?" her teacher asks.

1	2	3	4	5	6	7	8	9	10
11	12	13	14	15	16	17	18	19	20
21	22	23	24	25	26	27	28	29	30
31	32	33	34	35	36	37	38	39	40
41	42	43	44	45	46	47	48	49	50
51	52	53	54	55	56	57	58	59	60
61	62	63	64	65	66	67	68	69	70
71	72	73	74	75	76	77	78	79	80
81	82	83	84	85	86	87	88	89	90
91	92	93	94	95	96	97	98	99	100

FIGURE 4–3   *Emily's recording of the numbers 1–100*

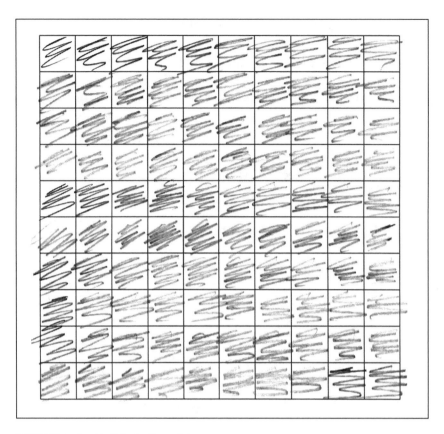

FIGURE 4–4 *Emily's shading of the squares*

Emily shows the hundreds chart she has created with numbers and then the one with shaded squares. "See," Emily declares, "they both are one hundred."

Beatrice has already completed a chart from 1 to 100, working across the chart from left to right, when she gets another blank chart. She begins with 101 (see Figure 4–5). She continues to record 101 through 120 correctly, but beginning with 121, follows a different pattern. She writes 1121 for 121 and continues this pattern through 1130 (130). On the next row she adds an additional 1 to form 11131 for 131.

When her teacher asks about her work, Beatrice responds, "I was following the pattern. I started with a one and zero and one [pointing to 101]. Then I needed two ones and a one [111]. Then I needed three ones [11131]. Oops, this doesn't look right. I think

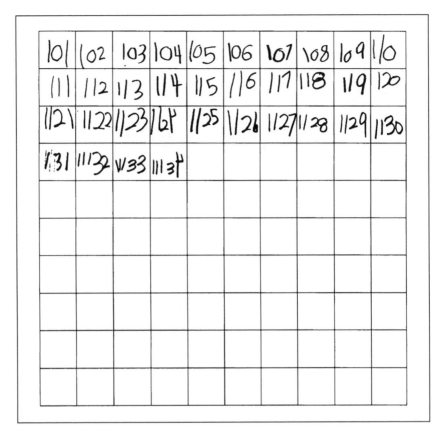

FIGURE 4–5   *Beatrice's work*

I should do this over." She erases the 11131 and records 131. "Is this right?" she asks her teacher. Upon receiving a positive response, Beatrice goes off to get a new blank grid and start over.

Providing time for children to explain their thinking is vital. It is not uncommon for students to discover errors as they express their ideas aloud. Learning that you can self-correct is a powerful idea, one that helps to build confidence and a sense of self-control.

Lee begins by writing 35 on his grid paper (Figure 4–6). Next he writes 40 and goes across the top row to 80, counting by fives. In the second row we see 85, 90, 95, 100, 100, 5, 100, 10, and so on. When he shows his work to his teacher he announces with pride, "I counted by fives."

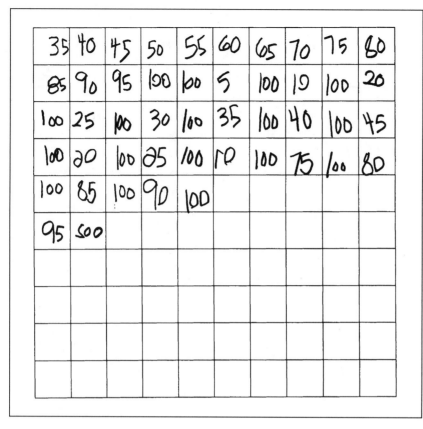

35	40	45	50	55	60	65	70	75	80
85	90	95	100	100	5	100	10	100	20
100	25	100	30	100	35	100	40	100	45
100	20	100	25	100	10	100	75	100	80
100	85	100	90	100					
95	500								

FIGURE 4–6 *Lee's work*

His teacher asks, "Can you read your work to me?"

Lee replies by counting from 35 to 110 by fives. Then he says, "Oops! I forgot one hundred and fifteen."

"How do you know you forgot one hundred fifteen?" asks his teacher.

Lee places his finger between 100 10 and 100 20. "It goes here," he explains.

Although Lee has also omitted 150 and 155, he clearly has an idea about how to say the numbers and how to count by fives. He is yet to use the conventional way of writing numbers, but his notation makes sense given the names for these numbers. Note that when he writes 200, he records it in the conventional manner, even though his two is reversed.

Writing numbers and using the hundreds boards help children see the patterns in our number system and how tens and ones are notated. Differentiating tens and ones within these numbers is a next step.

Marilyn Burns (2000) offers several tasks that help children look at tens and ones. The star game is one example. Learning to draw stars is exciting for first-grade students; they are proud of being able to make this shape. In Figure 4–7, Deanna shows us how many stars she can draw in one minute. After Deanna draws her stars in the allotted time, she creates groups of ten by putting a ring around ten stars at a time. Next, she records how many groups of ten and how many single stars she has. She prints 10 for each group circled and then double-checks by writing 1 through 8 next to the tens as she recounts her groups. Deanna knows she has

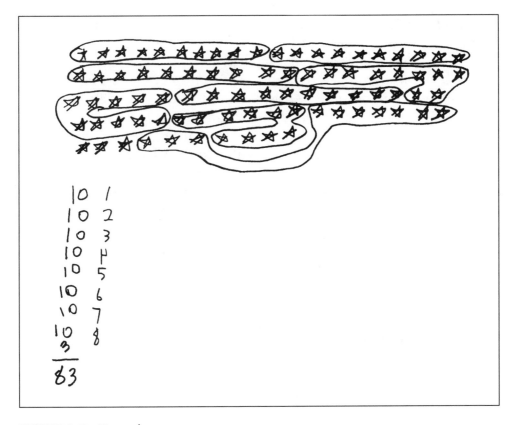

FIGURE 4–7   *Deanna's stars*

eight groups of ten stars. Next she counts aloud by tens to eighty, then adds, "One, two, three—eighty-three!"

Using Manipulative Models of Our Number System

Many educators advocate the use of concrete materials to build an understanding of our number system. Such materials can help children begin to link a group of objects with a number name and a written symbol. There are a variety of manipulative models, and teachers should understand the benefits and limitations of each. We need to think about how the different materials represent our number system and how they affect students' learning.

In some classrooms, Unifix cubes are the standard manipulatives for numbers. Initially, the students represent a number such as twenty-four by linking twenty-four cubes in a row. Within this model, through instructional activities, students learn to group the blocks in stacks of ten. Placing chips in bags or putting an elastic band around ten items, such as tongue depressors, are examples of similar models.

When children make the groups of ten themselves, the groups have more meaning. A disadvantage of these models, however, is that they don't extend well to greater numbers. Also, there is no way for the child to easily know if he has placed exactly ten blocks in each stack, ten chips in each bag, or ten sticks in each group. Students can check Unifix cube stacks by comparing their lengths. Yet neglecting to match end points, or making an initial stack of nine or eleven, can lead to undetected errors.

Teachers sometimes adopt other simple representations such as different-color chips or pennies, dimes, and dollars. It should be noted that these materials are not proportional; that is, the model for ten is not ten times as big as the model for one. Though the colors are attractive, there is no obvious reason why ten yellow chips should be traded for one blue chip. While different-color chips allow for flexible grouping (e.g., younger children can play three-for-one trading games) that expose students to the idea of one-to-many groupings while working with numbers they can recognize, the trading rule is arbitrary. While using units from our monetary system can reinforce or build ideas about money, they can be confusing (the penny is actually larger than a dime). The greatest disadvantage of nonproportional models is that they may emphasize the notion that mathematics doesn't make sense, that it's simply a bunch of rules.

Base ten blocks are probably the most well-known place-value material. They are proportional and students can line up the ten ones along the one ten to see the equivalent relationship. Similarly, ten tens can be arranged in the same shape as the hundred piece, and ten hundreds can be shown to be equivalent to the thousand piece. Once the equivalency is internalized, children trade without lining the pieces up or are able to simply take, for example, three tens and five ones, to show the number thirty-five. As such, these materials provide ready-made representations of tens, hundreds, and thousands, allowing students to model larger numbers quite easily.

There are some disadvantages to these materials. Students do not need to construct the larger pieces and therefore, young children may rotely get five tens and six ones to represent the number fifty-six, without truly understanding its equivalence to fifty-six ones. The ones are quite small, making them difficult to line up along a ten. If a child were counting forty-three ones, for example, and then trading to find their representation as tens and ones, a matching error could easily be made. Further, most teachers and curriculum materials emphasize the ten ones in a ten and the ten tens in a hundred without ever having students create the hundred piece from ones because it is too cumbersome.

Also, children may have difficulty visualizing how the next piece, representing ten thousand, should look. In fact, for some, the shapes of the pieces conjure up images of a point, a line, a plane, and a cube (Figure 4–8); it is impossible to imagine anything beyond the three-dimensional representation. While young students do not work with such numbers, an image of continuity is valuable.

The Digi-Block model of numbers is relatively new. The blocks are designed so that when ten singles are placed upright in a holder and then a second holder is placed on top of them, they form a new piece, a block-of-ten (see Figure 4–9). The block-of-ten looks exactly like the single block except that it is bigger. This process is referred to as packing (or unpacking, when

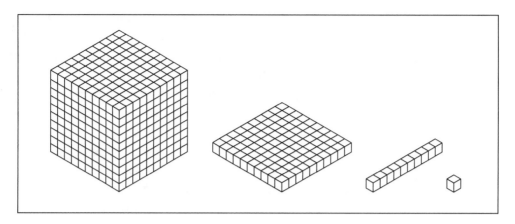

FIGURE 4–8   *Base ten pieces*

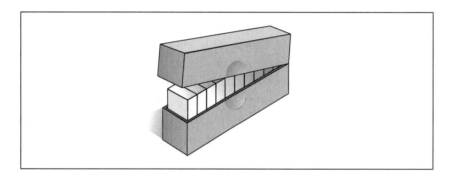

FIGURE 4–9   *Making a block-of-ten*

the procedure is reversed). Due to the unique design, the new block is formed only when there are exactly ten smaller blocks inside it. If there are fewer than ten, the holders fall apart. This feature allows students to self-check their work and eliminates a source of careless error.

The process can then be repeated. When ten blocks-of-ten are placed upright in a bigger holder and then covered, they form a block-of-one-hundred. A block-of-one-thousand may also be constructed. All four of the blocks look exactly alike except that they are of different size. This similarity makes it possible for students to visualize the continuity of numbers.

Packing the blocks is an active process that students enjoy. When a child packs 150 single blocks, she must first make the ten blocks-of-ten that go inside a block-of-one-hundred. This procedure makes it far more likely that the child will eventually understand that there are fifteen tens in 150.

There are drawbacks to the Digi-Block model, however. The initial unit is reasonably easy to manipulate, but larger blocks require a great deal of storage space. The fact that blocks-of-one-thousand contain ten blocks-of-one-hundred, each of which contain ten blocks-of-ten, each of which contain ten singles, is a wonderful model of our nested number system. The result, however, is that a block-of-one-thousand weighs about eighteen pounds!

Teachers may not have much say about the manipulative models available for use in their classrooms. But when the advantages and disadvantages of these models are understood, teachers can make better use of their materials and identify characteristics of manipulatives that may lead to less-well-developed ideas. Questions for teachers to think about when evaluating models of the number system include:

Does the model make the relationships among the different places obvious?

Does the child construct the representation of the different places or are they ready-made?

Is it clear that the numbers represented by the model could easily continue?

Are the pieces easy to manipulate?

Is there a self-checking component to the model?

Is the model proportional?

Is the model easy to use?

Is it easy to store?

Is the material attractive?

Does the model support investigation of other groupings/bases?

While shown to be helpful, use of a concrete model does not necessarily lead to understanding. These materials can be used rotely by children, and the relationships among objects, the concrete representation of that number of objects, and the numeral for that quantity may not be fully understood. Consider Ramie's work (Figure 4–10.) This first grader was asked to make a set of Unifix cubes equivalent to the number of stones in a bag. Ramie counted the number of stones in the bag by ones and arrived at the correct number, twenty-six. Next, Ramie counted twenty-six cubes and then grouped them in two stacks of ten, with six loose cubes remaining. While working, Ramie placed the stacks of ten to the right of the loose cubes, and then drew them in that orientation. She recorded the number of loose blocks and the number of tens in that order and wrote the numeral 62. The following conversation with her teacher ensued.

TEACHER: HOW MANY STONES DID YOU COUNT?
    RAMIE: Twenty-six.
TEACHER: WHAT NUMBER DOES THIS SHOW *[pointing to the 62]*?
    RAMIE: The number of stones.
TEACHER: CAN YOU READ ME THE NUMBER?
    RAMIE: Sixty-two.
TEACHER: IS THAT THE NUMBER OF STONES?
    RAMIE: Sort of . . . uh, I think. It's the number of tens and ones.

Before this conversation, the teacher never thought about this subtle difference between a physical model and our number

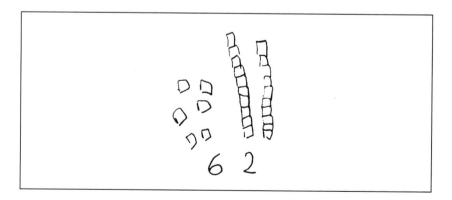

FIGURE 4–10 *Ramie's representation*

system. The concrete model shows twenty-six regardless of whether the tens are to the right or to the left of the ones. To record the digits within our conventional system, however, the tens must be to the left of the ones.

Finally, it is essential not to limit mathematical thinking through inflexible use of base ten materials. Place-value charts can be helpful, but it is important not to rigidly impose the separation of tens and ones. For example, imagine finding 36 + 14. Many children are taught to represent each number on a place-value chart with the tens put in the tens column and the ones in the ones column. The original numbers are then forgotten, as the columns are treated separately. When teachers stipulate use of such a procedure, they may preclude a child from noting that the four ones from fourteen could join with the thirty-six to make forty. Then, one more ten is fifty.

Thus, as students explore isolating the tens and ones within a number, it is important that they retain their number sense. An intuitive feel for how big numbers are and a visual sense of where they are in a number line or on a hundreds board is particularly important when learning to add and subtract with larger numbers.

Learning Procedures to Add and Subtract

Many of us were taught to add (and subtract) in the same way. We were instructed to add the ones, "carry" the tens, add the tens, and so on. This procedure is recognized as a traditional or conventional algorithm for addition. While this method is efficient, it was often learned by rote, and some of us used it without any real understanding of what we were doing.

Exclusive use of this algorithm leads to reliance on conducting a series of steps rather than on using good number sense and reasoning. Thus, errors (see example in Figure 4–11) are not uncommon. Teachers often look at such work and wonder, "How can he think this is correct?" or "Didn't she even look at the numbers?" Unfortunately, this technique encourages children to examine the numbers in parts, not as wholes. Given the equation 28 + 17 they think about ones and tens, not about the numbers 28 and 17. Further, when a multistep procedure is conducted rotely, it is easy to make an error in one of the steps.

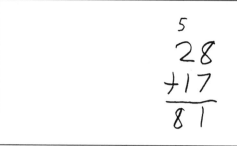

FIGURE 4–11   *Common student error*

In lieu of a teacher-directed singular approach, the National Council of Teachers of Mathematics in its *Standards 2000* suggests that children be given opportunities to construct their own strategies, become comfortable with more than one approach, and develop a clear understanding of the techniques that they use (NCTM 2000). Discussion and representation of computational techniques are vital to these goals. Students need to be able to explain their thinking and follow the ideas of others. They need to develop recording schemes that support their ability to keep track of and to document their thinking.

A second-grade teacher poses the following problem to her students: *There are 17 seashells in Maria's bucket. She puts 23 more shells in the bucket. How many shells are in the bucket now?* The children solve the problem on their own. It is early January and their work demonstrates a diverse set of skills and understandings.

Kurt and Danielle are still working with ones. Kurt counts out a group of seventeen cubes and then a group of twenty-three cubes. He puts the cubes together and counts them all to find the total. He records only the numeral 40 on his paper. Danielle also forms the two groups of cubes, but she counts on from twenty-three to find the total. She records the answer and her strategy—"I counted them"—on her paper. The teacher notes that Kurt has used the counting-on strategy when working with smaller numbers, but he did not use it today with these larger numbers. She knows that it is not unusual for children to revert to a counting-all strategy when confronted with larger numbers.

Several of the children use base ten blocks. First Jasmine gets two tens and three ones (to represent twenty-three), and then she gathers a ten and seven ones (for seventeen). She counts, "ten, twenty, thirty," and then counts on by ones. Note that her recording (see Figure 4–12) shows both how she represented each addend and how she arrived at the total.

Cam also uses the tens and ones pieces to show the numbers seventeen and twenty-three. Once both numbers are represented, he moves all of the tens to the left and all of the ones to the right. Cam also counts aloud—"ten, twenty, thirty"—and finishes by counting his ten single pieces. He adds mentally to arrive at his final answer, and represents his thinking (Figure 4–13) by drawing the three ten pieces as part of his addition equation.

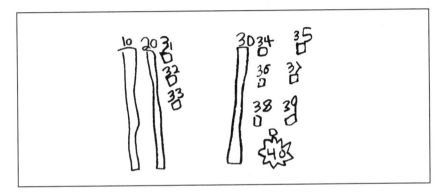

FIGURE 4–12   *Jasmine's work*

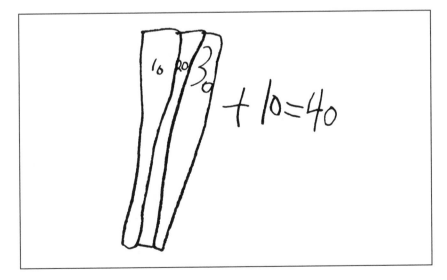

FIGURE 4–13   *Cam's work*

Many of the children work without materials. Roberto, Maxie, and Denise add the tens and the ones, beginning with the tens, and then combine these subtotals. Roberto and Maxie draw lines to show how they are combining the numbers. Roberto records his work horizontally and Maxie works vertically. Note that Denise thinks similarly, but only records equations (see Figure 4–14).

Andy uses a traditional algorithm (see Figure 4–15). His teacher takes note of his progress and a conversation ensues.

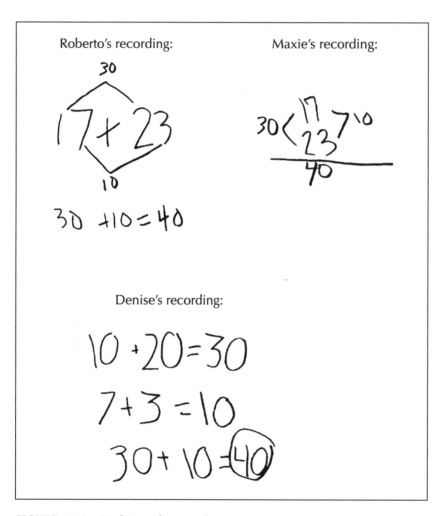

FIGURE 4–14 *Working with tens and ones*

FIGURE 4–15   *Andy's use of traditional algorithm*

TEACHER: THAT LOOKS INTERESTING. CAN YOU TELL ME WHAT YOU ARE
DOING?

ANDY: Oh sure. See, you just do the ones and then the tens.

TEACHER: WHAT DOES THIS MEAN? *[pointing to the one indicating the
ten ones that were regrouped]*.

ANDY: It's the ten I got over here *[pointing to the ones column]*.
It's like a shortcut.

TEACHER: HMM, WHERE DID YOU LEARN THAT?

ANDY: My father showed me. Cool, huh?

Based on his explanation, the teacher believes that Andy
understands what he is doing, and thus she is comfortable with
his use of this approach. It is common for parents to teach their
children this algorithm, if it has not yet been introduced in
school. Because of this, it is important that parents be included
in conversations about our teaching techniques, and the need for
children to understand the concepts behind algorithms rather
than apply them by rote.

When a student introduces a "carrying over" approach to his
or her classmates, perhaps during a debriefing session, some children may adopt its use as is or integrate it with their own techniques. Upon learning of this procedure, Maxie (who worked
vertically, connecting numbers with lines) began incorporating

the use of a 1 in the tens column to show the regrouped ones (see Figure 4–16). When explaining her work to her teacher she said, "I wanted to use Andy's way."

Zelda's thinking is somewhat different (Figure 4–17). She does not total the tens and ones separately, but instead adds the three (from twenty-three) to seventeen to get twenty, and then adds the remaining twenty. When Zelda explains her approach she says, "I wanted to get to an easy number, so I took the three from over here and put it with the seventeen."

The search for compatible, friendly numbers or efficient ways to combine and separate numbers that are easy to work with develops over time. Those of us who learned a traditional approach were often told to "look for tens" in the ones column. This is a similar way of thinking, but unfortunately, it was limited to use in one column at a time. Looking for number relationships within the problem as a whole as well as within columns is productive, demonstrates flexibility, and builds number sense.

One second-grade teacher encourages his students to think about the different ways in which numbers can be decomposed.

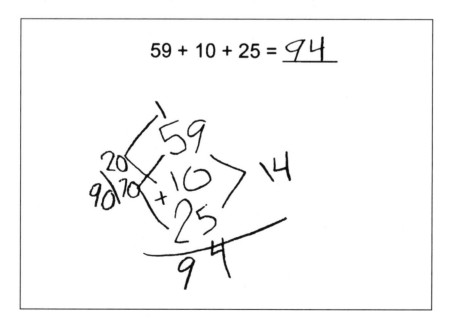

FIGURE 4–16   *Maxie incorporates Andy's way*

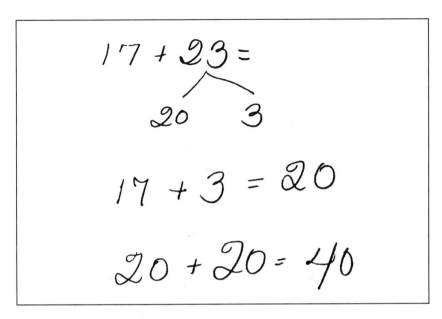

FIGURE 4–17   *Zelda's work*

Each day when the children note the number of days they have been in school, they are then asked to find different equations equal to that number. Early in the year, the teacher gives them a worksheet to ignite their thinking (see Figure 4–18). By midyear, his students use mental arithmetic to find examples.

Over time, as students' number sense grows, they are able to work more flexibly with numbers. For example, when Luanna adds seventy-seven and thirty-five, she works first with seventy-five and twenty-five (see Figure 4–19). "I like to look for a hundred," she explains. Such flexibility in thinking rarely develops from exclusive work with a traditional algorithm or from restricted use of base ten materials.

By the end of the year, these second-grade students are looking at the expression 47 + 15. They are asked to find the sum using mental arithmetic. The following conversation takes place.

EMILLIO: Forty plus ten is fifty and seven plus five is twelve. So that makes sixty-two.

GLEN: I did it that way too. *[Several other heads nod to signify that they used this technique as well.]*

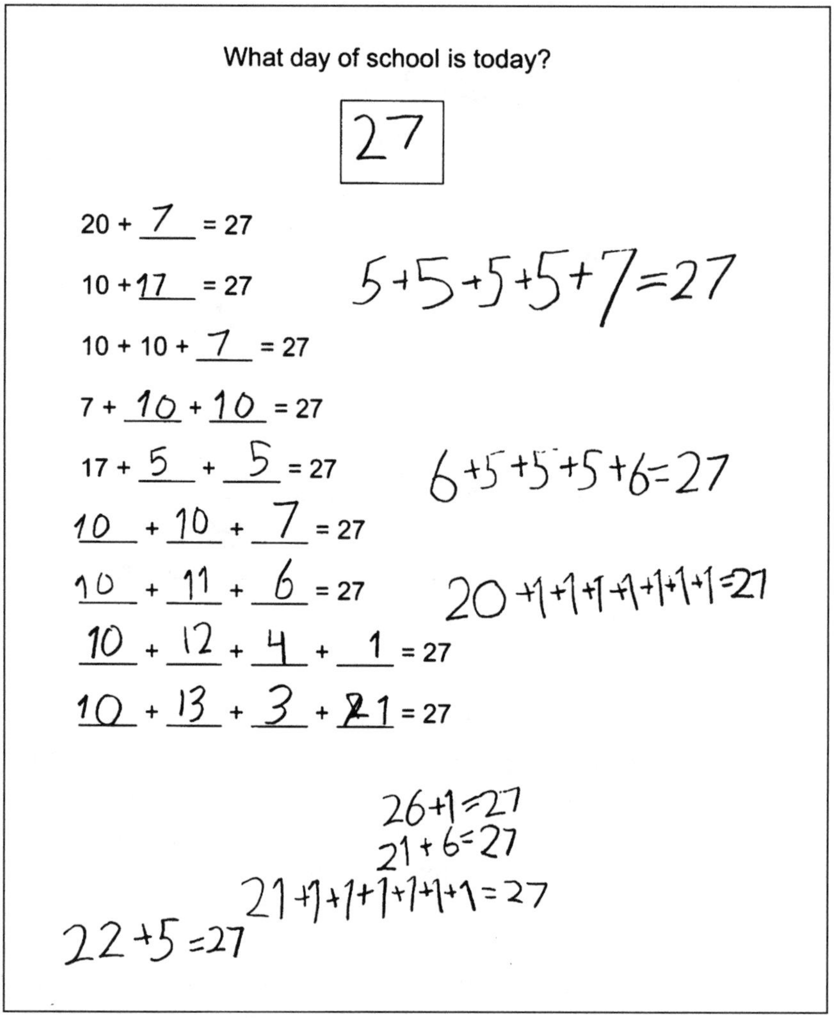

What day of school is today?

$$\boxed{27}$$

20 + __7__ = 27

10 + __17__ = 27 $5+5+5+5+7=27$

10 + 10 + __7__ = 27

7 + __10__ + __10__ = 27

17 + __5__ + __5__ = 27 $6+5+5+5+6=27$

__10__ + __10__ + __7__ = 27

__10__ + __11__ + __6__ = 27 $20+1+1+1+1+1+1+1=27$

__10__ + __12__ + __4__ + __1__ = 27

__10__ + __13__ + __3__ + __1__ = 27

$$26+1=27$$
$$21+6=27$$
$$21+1+1+1+1+1+1=27$$
$$22+5=27$$

FIGURE 4–18   *Decomposing the number of the day*

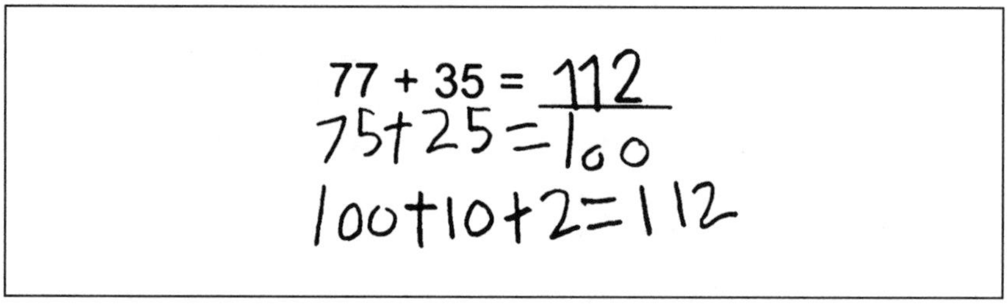

$$77 + 35 = \underline{112}$$
$$75+25=100$$
$$100+10+2=112$$

FIGURE 4–19   *Luanna's work*

RITA: Well, seven and three is ten, so you take three from the fifteen and add it to forty-seven and you have fifty. Then there's twelve left and so you have sixty-two.

LUANNA: I took five from forty-seven and put it with the fifteen. So then I thought, "forty-two and twenty is sixty-two."

TEACHER: DOES ANYONE HAVE ANOTHER WAY?

MIKEL: I started at forty-seven and counted up five on my fingers. [*Mikel counts aloud to fifty-two. Each time he says a number, he extends a finger on his right hand.*] Then ten more is sixty-two.

PAM: Where did the five come from?

NED: I split the fifteen into five and ten.

PAM: Oh, I see.

It is clear that these students have developed a variety of ways to think about this problem. They have acquired an understanding about numbers and addition that allows them to compute accurately and with flexibility. They engage easily in discourse about their strategies and listen to one another's ideas.

Note that it is possible to think with greater flexibility when examples are written horizontally. The vertical presentation, at least for those who learned the traditional approach, appears to automatically stimulate its use without the student first thinking about the actual numbers involved. The disadvantage of this approach can be seen when children automatically add the ones, the tens, and the hundreds to solve, for example, 345 + 200, when such an equation could easily be worked out using mental arithmetic. Or when they fail to realize that 399 + 76 can be found easily by identifying 400 + 76 and then subtracting 1.

Computational fluency results from the intentional use of varied computational techniques. It requires teachers to adopt classroom practices that weave mathematical ideas with skill development.

Teacher Reflection

When I first began teaching ten years ago, I taught my students to add and subtract in the traditional ways. They spent a lot of time using base ten blocks and I was never really sure what to do for those students who weren't able to transfer their processes to paper and pencil. Then I took a summer course that helped me to understand that the traditional algorithm was only one strategy of many that could be used. I began to think about what experiences children would need in order to invent their own ways to add and subtract. I decided that I would never use a single approach again.

At first, it was a bit scary. What if my students didn't learn efficient techniques? What would their parents say about my new ideas? What would the third-grade teachers think?

Over time, my confidence in this way of teaching grew. On a given day, children are working with both concrete and abstract representations. Some children are counting numbers by ones using Unifix cubes, some are drawing pictures of tens and ones, and some are using their own paper-and-pencil techniques based on their understanding of numbers. Small- and large-group discussions are a key place for learning. Over the course of the year, the children's techniques change. They learn from our work with the hundreds board, from our composing and decomposing number activities, and from each other.

I have found that when children aren't making progress, it is important to help them do so. Right now I have a student who loves to draw. She carefully draws pictures of base ten blocks when solving problems with two-digit numbers. She then counts up her tens and her ones. After seeing this same strategy for much of the year, I realize that she probably doesn't still need to make those drawings. I need to intervene. In a game-like way, I can ask her to try to picture the blocks in her mind, but not draw them.

Sometimes parents don't understand why their children aren't learning the traditional algorithm as *the* way to solve addition and subtraction problems. When I've taken the time to show the parents samples of their children's work and the progression of their understanding over time, they breathe much easier. At open house, I often demonstrate a lesson, calling on parents to mentally solve an addition problem. As parents share their strategies, they begin to see the variety of ways that people look at numbers.

I love when the number system comes alive for children. I love that my students are developing their own ways of thinking about numbers and their own ways of recording their work. When I tried to explain a strategy that all children should use, I felt like I lost the class. When I ask the children to become actively involved, they are excited to explore, to create and modify strategies, and to learn. They have confidence in their own thinking and abilities because they build from their own ideas.

For older generations, computational fluency often means accurate performance of specified procedures. There is much greater variety in today's classrooms, and a fuller understanding of what it means to be fluent in addition or subtraction. By the end of second grade children should be able to use efficient strategies that they can produce easily and accurately, record effectively, and explain meaningfully. This requires knowledge of basic facts and an understanding of the number system. It includes acquisition of more than one approach that can be selected on the basis of the specific problem or numbers.

Such fluency is developed over time and is supported through children's representations and discourse. Once acquired, students not only have powerful mathematical skills, they view themselves as creators and doers of mathematics.

5

Collecting, Representing, and Interpreting Data

Data collection has been an interest of primary teachers since Mary Baratta-Lorton first published *Mathematics Their Way* (1976). Numerous K–2 classrooms prominently display graphic representations that help organize attendance, dismissal, and lunch counts. These daily routines demonstrate how important the collection and display of data are in our lives. Some teachers provide students with a question as they enter the classroom, such as, *Are you the youngest in your family?* The children then place their name cards, pictures, or blocks in the yes pile or the no pile.

Through such investigations, young students begin to understand that they can both find and communicate information in data, charts, and graphs. They recognize the one-to-one correspondence between themselves and the graphical representations. As the questions become more complex, the children have opportunities to compare parts of the data, resulting in such conclusions as "More children take the bus than get a ride." They are also able to draw conclusions about the data as a whole (e.g., "Most children are having a school lunch"). They can begin to apply the data to new situations when responding to such questions as, "Do you think this data would be different if we asked the same question—'What time do you go to bed?'—of fourth-grade students?"

While significant, such data activities are limited if the teacher chooses the questions and the ways in which the data are displayed. Consider the teacher comments below.

Teacher Reflection

Did you ever have one of those students whose persistent questions reverberate in your mind long after the day is over? The kind of child whose intonation borders on annoyance, but whose words you just can't shake? You want to dismiss his or her pestering, but you know deep down inside the child is saying something truly profound. I've had several of those students over the years and when I move my teacher ego aside, I learn a great deal from their insights.

When I close my eyes and think back about work with data in my classroom, I can hear a small nagging voice whisper to a classmate, "I bet she's going to make a graph about this." The look of agreement and simultaneous discontent on the students' faces tells all. These young children are already growing weary of an aspect of mathematics that should entice, but instead, has lost their interest.

In my early years of teaching I always thought that having the children participate in a graphing activity was a nice diversion from our regular math lessons. I thought it was fun to think of an interesting question and then to identify a clever way for my students to record their individual responses. Often I had predetermined the way the graph would look by meticulously cutting out apples, spiders, flowers, or some other related icon for their use and by carefully preprinting labels such as, "I like Red Delicious apples" or "I'm afraid of spiders."

I didn't realize that by taking over these tasks, I was the only one really doing the graphing activity. Sure, the children wrote their names on a precut piece of paper to add to the growing bar graph, but that is all they really did. It was only after hearing that nagging voice about how I would be making another graph that I began to think about who was really engaged in the work. My young students realized long before I did that they were getting little from this exercise.

But what do I want for my students with respect to data?

In this honest reflection, the primary-grade teacher helps us think about the key ideas related to data with which K–2 students can and should grapple. We have learned that it is not enough, nor is it very stimulating, for the teacher to be the only person identifying questions to which responses are collected. We must help children to develop their own questions and to represent their findings in ways that make sense to them.

In addition to providing ample opportunities for children to generate questions for surveys and to collect and record data, we should encourage our students to share their findings. By seeing the variety of ways in which classmates display data, children learn how to interpret graphic representations made by others. They broaden their understanding of the data and begin to link different representations of the same ideas. They engage in mathematical discussions that help to build a community of learners.

Field Trip Surveys

Being able to formulate a question is an important first step in the data-collection process. When children have the opportunity to identify a question, they can choose one that interests them and their classmates. Once a question is identified, they need to think about the best way to collect their data. Who will respond to their survey? How will they be sure they have included each of their classmates? As students begin to collect the data, they sometimes find that their questions are not clear and may decide to revise their thinking. Sometimes, once all of the data are collected, children find that they are not sure how to organize it and return to a simpler question.

Consider this example from a first-grade class whose teacher has been thinking for several years about the goals of data activities. She has decided she wants her students to collect data for a real purpose. She thinks this approach will be more meaningful to them and will offer new learning opportunities.

Each spring her class attends a field trip to the Boston Public Garden and State House. In the spring, the children spend several weeks learning about the life cycles of chicks and ducks. Simultaneously, they pursue an author study of the works of Robert McCloskey. A field trip to the Public Garden is a perfect opportunity for these children living near metropolitan Boston to learn more about the city. Tracing the steps that Mr. and Mrs. Mallard take in the book *Make Way for Ducklings* is one part of a lively and age-appropriate integrated unit of study for these first graders.

On the day after the students return from their much-anticipated field trip, they gather for a math lesson and their teacher tells them about a questionnaire she received from the field trip organizers.

TEACHER: YESTERDAY WE WENT ON A FIELD TRIP. AS WE WERE LEAVING, ONE OF THE DOCENTS FROM THE STATE HOUSE GAVE ME THIS FORM. I WAS WONDERING IF YOU COULD HELP ME FILL IT OUT. IT ASKS QUESTIONS LIKE, "HOW MANY STUDENTS ATTENDED TODAY'S TRIP?"; "DID YOU FIND THE GUIDES INFORMATIVE?"; "WAS THE TRIP AGE-APPROPRIATE?" WHY DO YOU THINK THEY WANT TO KNOW THESE THINGS?

JOSH: Do they want to know if we liked the trip? I liked the trip!

LILLY: I think they get so many kids that it's hard to count, and they want to know how many kids ride the swan boats. I liked riding the swan boats.

ZED: Maybe they don't think we learned anything.

TEACHER: IT SEEMS LIKE YOU ALL HAVE A LOT TO SAY ABOUT OUR TRIP. I WONDER IF WE COULD GIVE THE ORGANIZERS MORE INFORMA-TION IF YOU TAKE SOME SURVEYS. WHAT KIND OF QUESTIONS DO YOU THINK MIGHT BE HELPFUL FOR THEM?

LUANNE: Did you like going on the swan boats? Yes or No.

TORY: Did you like the bus ride? I didn't. I thought it was really long.

PEDRO: Did you feed the ducks?

TEACHER: I CAN TELL YOU HAVE MANY HELPFUL IDEAS. WHY DON'T YOU EACH GET SOME PAPER AND GET STARTED.

The students then scurry off to obtain paper and writing utensils, formulate and print their questions, and begin to collect data. It is May, and much prior work has provided these first graders with a solid foundation for this activity. General classroom expectations are clear and the children are familiar with formulating survey questions.

The children all seem able to craft a reasonable question, organize their paper prior to collecting data, and engage in a meaningful quest of inquiry with their classmates. In less than forty minutes, the children seem satisfied with their progress and ready for the next step.

Ready-made forms listing all of the students' names are available to students who want them. These lists were not available earlier in the year, because the teacher wanted the students to recognize the importance of keeping track of persons being surveyed and to suggest their own techniques for doing so. It was during a class discussion that one of the students suggested that a preprinted list would be helpful. Another student, building on this idea, suggested that the list be "like the one you [the teacher] keep on your clipboard." Since the suggestion was made, copies of the list are kept in an acetate holder that hangs at the back of the room, so that they are easily available at all times.

Many children reach for one of these lists to help them collect their data. As you can see from Blake's work (Figure 5–1), the list is only a starting point. Blake poses the question, "Did you like going on Miss Mallard?" (There are bronze sculptures of McCloskey's duck characters in the Boston Public Garden. The children were excited to see them and eagerly took turns sitting on the mallards' backs.) Blake puts a check mark beside the names of classmates who respond positively, an X when the response is negative, and a question mark for Denise, who was absent due to an important family event in New York. Once he makes a mark for the response, he records *yes* or *no* as well. This

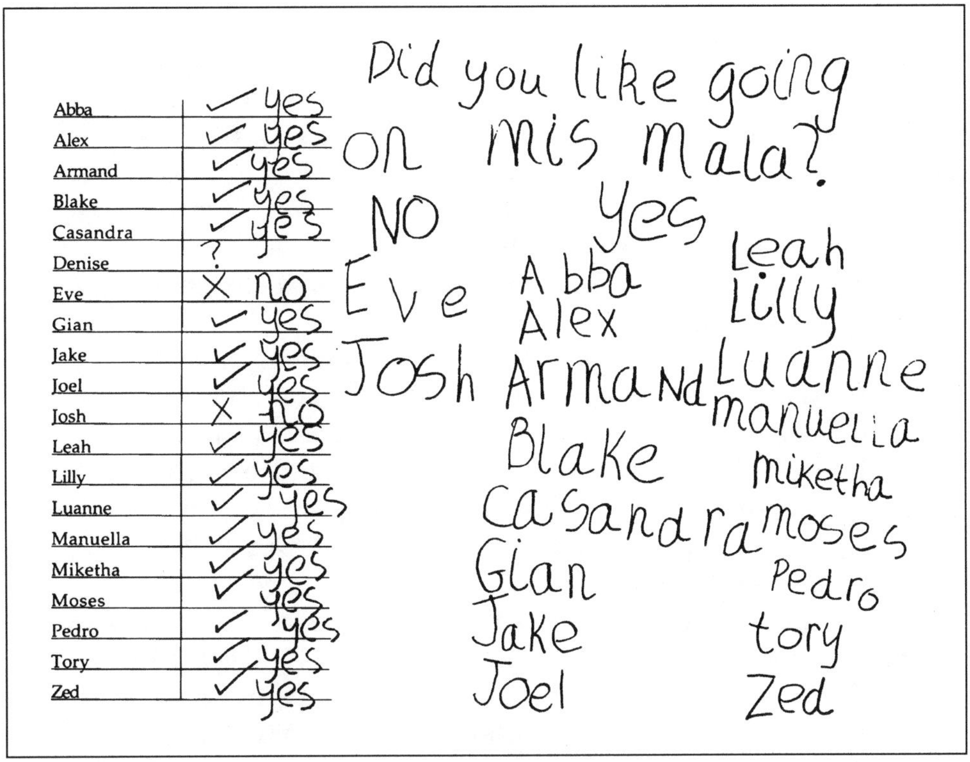

FIGURE 5–1 *Blake's work*

second step seems to solidify the responses. After he successfully collects all of the data, he reorganizes it. He makes two columns, one for *yes* and one for *no*, and then carefully prints each classmate's name under the proper heading. He does not include Denise, because data on a person not attending the field trip "didn't really fit."

Crafting a question and collecting data are two critical aspects of this investigation. Once children have their questions and data, their teacher asks them to interpret it in some way. She sets up the premise that the children are going to send this information to the field trip organizers. She asks, "How do you think you can describe what you have found out to the people who set up our field trip? What did you learn from your survey that you think they will find helpful?" Her hope is that the children can convey their findings in a clear and concise manner.

The teacher recognizes that this task will not be easy for her students. She knows that they can easily identify the number of yes and no responses, but for some time she has wondered if first graders can go beyond this in some meaningful way. She has asked them to interpret data before, but never to think about the viewer's perspective. It is not that she expects her young students to grasp every aspect of this idea, but she hopes that by setting this challenge, she can help them to move beyond a rudimentary listing of quantifiable facts.

Luanne's survey question is "Did you like going on the field trip?" She carefully listed yes or no next to each name. She even included Denise's response—a yes—followed by the explanation that "She said that [had she been there] it would be nice." Luanne responds to the teacher's further probe by explaining why she picked her question (see Figure 5–2). She writes about her own experience on the day of the field trip: "I wanted to know this question because I had a hard time. Because I lost my tooth. Everyone said yes! And no one said no. And altogether I had 20." This brief synopsis reveals that Luanne can express why she thought her question was interesting and that she can account for all twenty of her classmates, including herself.

I Wontid to no this cwshtin
becos I had a hard Time.
becos I lost my tooth.
Evry one Sead yes!
and noone sead no!
and all tugther I had 20.

FIGURE 5–2 *Luanne's work*

Keeping track and establishing a one-to-one match with each respondent is a critical aspect of data collection.

Casandra too, writes a summary statement (see Figure 5–3). She notes that everyone liked looking at the ceiling pattern in the State House, except for Denise, who was in New York and unable to see it. Casandra also makes a new representation of her data. She shows nineteen stick figures looking up (see Figure 5–4). Note that their mouths are open with awe and that an arrow points upward over each figure. Casandra also provides a key to let the reader know what the arrow indicates. The one stick figure standing alone has a line for a mouth. As Casandra explains, "This means that the person is not looking." This figure represents Denise.

Sometimes children generate an interesting question for their survey that can't be answered with a simple yes or no. Lilly begins with the question, "What did you like best about the field trip?" After collecting a few responses she limits her question by including two choices: "the Swan Boats or having lunch?" When asked about this revision she explains, "It was too hard if everyone gave a different answer." Once the data to her revised question is

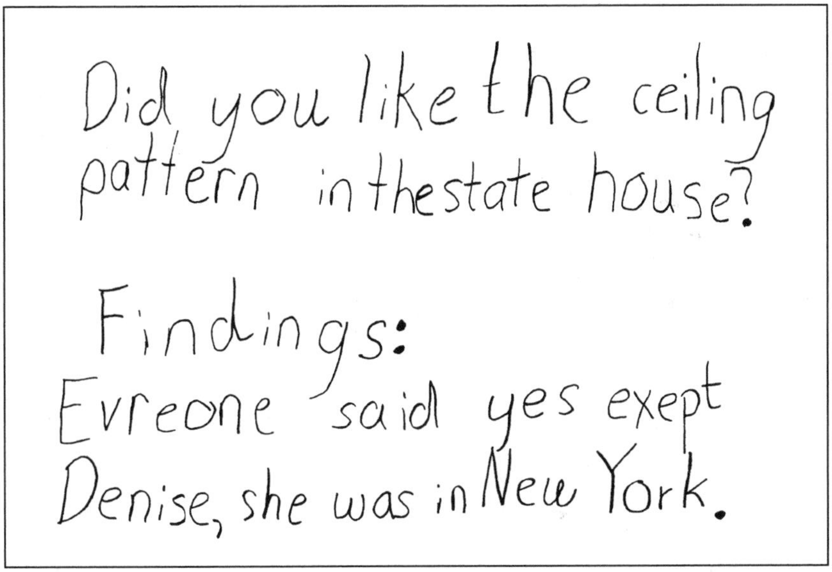

Did you like the ceiling pattern in the state house?

Findings:
Evreone said yes exept Denise, she was in New York.

FIGURE 5–3 *Casandra's summary statement*

FIGURE 5–4 *Casandra's representation of data*

collected, she represents the responses with links. She makes three chains: one with twelve links, for those who liked the swan boats best, one with seven links, for those who chose lunch, and one with one link, to stand for Denise. It is important to have a variety of materials for students to use when they represent data. Not all children are comfortable with pencil and paper recordings and it is important to support a variety of perspectives and learning styles.

Although Denise was absent for the trip, she had been with her class throughout the unit and it was important that she not be further left out of the activity. Perhaps because she did not have preconceived notions about the trip, she asks the same open-ended question with which Lilly began. Denise records each of the different responses and then she puts an X by her own name (see Figure 5–5). On a second sheet (see Figure 5–6), Denise writes, "I found out . . ." under which she lists the nine different responses and the number of children that belong in each category. On the right side of her paper she writes, "findings" and concludes that "more people said swan boats."

Children have a way of adding their own personalities to their work. Luanne's survey example lets her teacher know how

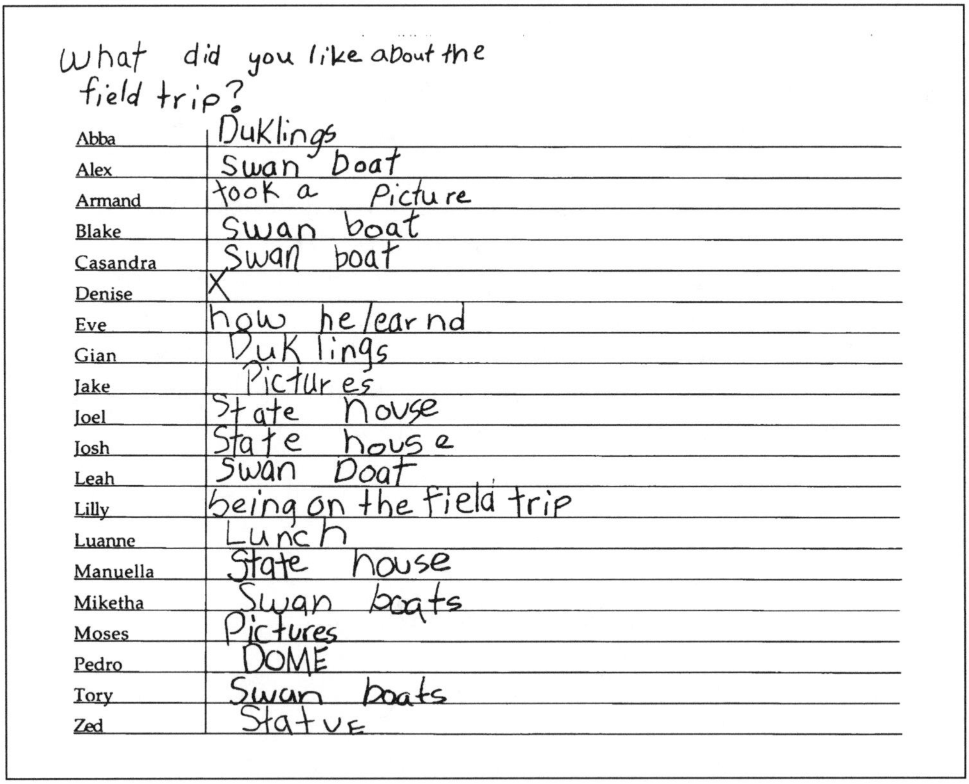

What did you like about the
field trip?

Abba	Duklings
Alex	Swan boat
Armand	took a Picture
Blake	Swan boat
Casandra	Swan boat
Denise	X
Eve	how he learnd
Gian	Duklings
Jake	Pictures
Joel	State house
Josh	State house
Leah	Swan boat
Lilly	being on the field trip
Luanne	Lunch
Manuella	State house
Miketha	Swan boats
Moses	Pictures
Pedro	DOME
Tory	Swan boats
Zed	Statue

FIGURE 5–5   *Denise's recording of responses*

I found out...   findings

Swan boats 6
Pictures   3   more people
learnd somthing 1   said swan boats
State house 3
Duklings 2
Lunch 1
being on the field trip 1
DOME 1
Statue 1

FIGURE 5–6   *Denise's findings*

important it was to her that she had lost a tooth. Casandra's arrows and awed ceiling gazers remind the teacher of her dramatic flair. Denise's ability to conduct a meaningful survey even though she was not present for the trip is consistent with her conscientious style.

In Alex's work, we learn about his humor and honesty. He asks, "Were you tired at the end of our field trip?" He records a yes or no by each name as well as a question mark for those students who weren't sure. His summary statement (see Figure 5–7) records the number of different responses. He then tells us, "We all had fun but many of us were tired." His final, "P.S. I'm still tired" captures his spirit and indicates clearly why this question

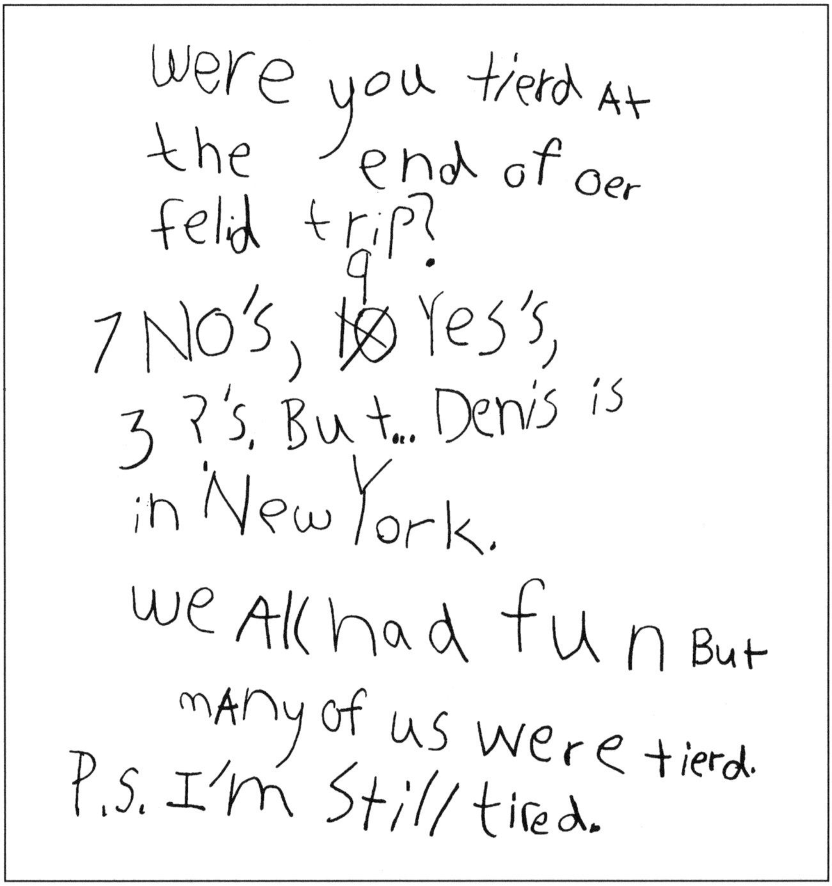

FIGURE 5–7 *Alex's summary statement*

was of interest to him. He then chooses to convey his data in a drawing (Figure 5–8). In his creative depiction, note the blank outline to represent the absent Denise and the way he combines features of the tired and the nontired to represent the unsure. Adding sixteen-ton bricks to the feet of his exhausted peers makes his point clear. Field trips can be both exhilarating and exhausting for teachers and students alike!

This culminating work with data showed just how much these first-grade students had learned during the year and that they were quite capable of meeting their teacher's challenge.

FIGURE 5–8   *Alex's representation of the data*

Among them they demonstrated the ability to organize their data into categories, to represent data in different ways, and to write summational statements. The creativity and variety in their work would not have been so evident if the teacher had provided the survey questions and the mechanisms for representing the results. Because the children were interested in their questions, they were more invested in the responses. Many students chose to represent the data in more than one way and to comment on their findings. At a class discussion that followed, they were eager to share their work with their classmates.

This project clearly shows that first-grade students can be involved in sophisticated investigations about data. What can we expect of kindergarten children?

Counting Ourselves

Our youngest students show a natural curiosity for data investigations. In most kindergarten classrooms, students are encouraged to participate in graphing experiences, often as part of their morning meetings when the number of students present is determined. Children naturally want to know that others care about whether or not they are present. When each child attaches a snap cube to a growing train of connected cubes, students can easily build a model to represent those who are present. While first graders focus a great deal of energy on making sure they have each and every child in their class represented in their surveys, kindergartners begin by working hard to identify themselves in a larger sea of information.

Over time students discover the relationships among the number of students present, the number of students absent, and the total number of students in the class. This total is an important piece of information for five and six year olds. Being able to recognize oneself as a member of a group is personally gratifying and mathematically significant. Ideas involving one-to-one correspondence, keeping track of a count, finding a total, and using an icon to represent oneself are developmentally appropriate and important tasks for this age group.

In the kindergarten unit Counting Ourselves and Others, developed by TERC (Economopoulos and Russell 1998), students are asked to count the number of people in their class. Following the counting process, each student creates his or her own representation showing the number of students. This activity is suggested for use after the midpoint in the year, long after children have begun exploring ideas about data with daily attendance routines and yes/no survey questions.

On the day when the children in one kindergarten class are asked to represent the number of students in their class, all of them know that the total is twenty-one. The challenge for them is to represent this data. Most children write numbers or draw pictures of children. Opal writes the numerals from 1 to 21 (Figure 5–9). Misha also writes these numerals, but includes a large 21 to indicate the total number (Figure 5–10).

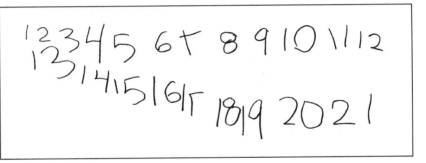

FIGURE 5–9   *Opal's work*

FIGURE 5–10   *Misha's work*

Amy draws people (see Figure 5–11). She recounts several times as she works. After she draws the last figure, she goes back and writes the numerals 1 through 21, each corresponding to one of the figures in her drawing. When asked about her work, she replies, "I drew a picture to show how many people are in our room. Then I counted and drew the numbers to be sure." The need to double-check or verify their work is evidently important to these children.

Tika also draws pictures of his classmates, and begins to label them by name. Tiring of this, he switches to recording only first initials (Figure 5–12). His figures continue to demonstrate quite a bit of detail, however, until he gets to the final figure, drawn in the lower right corner. But even in this drawing, facial features are identified. In most cases, he differentiates the hair of boys and girls. A few special details are included as well. John gets a hat, because "he loves hats." The S for Sandi is placed on the figure "just like superman."

FIGURE 5–11 *Amy's work*

FIGURE 5–12 *Tika's work*

Adam uses names as well. He copies a class list of names written in alphabetical order (Figure 5–13) and adds twenty-one circles as a second form of representation.

Ivan begins by writing 21 on his paper. Then he draws twenty-one noses (see Figure 5–14). In one of their previous activities, the children discussed counting noses as a way to count the number of children in class. That activity did not include representation, but Ivan clearly remembered the discussion and connected it to this investigation. Celeste's work (Figure 5–15) shows a more abstract form of representation. Referring to her illustration, she explains, "I drew [twenty-one] kisses and hugs."

Almost all of the children are successful with this activity. However, Larry's work (Figure 5–16) reminds us of how easily influenced, distracted, or confused some children presented with a task of this sort can be. Larry's display shows twelve figures or objects. His teacher asks him about his work.

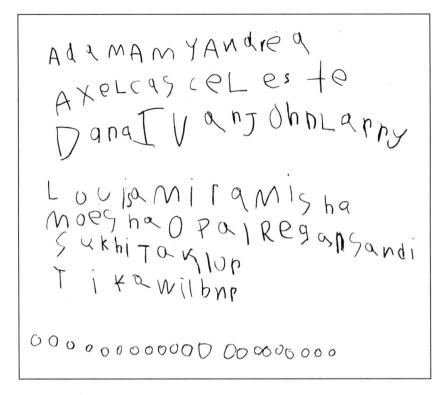

FIGURE 5–13   *Adam's work*

FIGURE 5–14   *Ivan's work*

TEACHER: WHAT CAN YOU TELL ME ABOUT YOUR DRAWING?

LARRY: I don't know. I just made it.

TEACHER: WHY DID WE MAKE THESE REPRESENTATIONS?

LARRY: Because, because we count how many people are in our class.

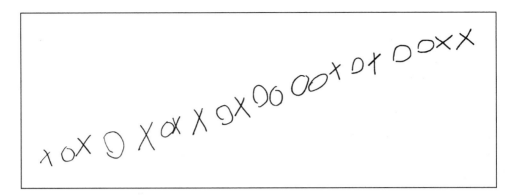

FIGURE 5–15   *Celeste's work*

FIGURE 5–16   *Larry's work*

TEACHER: SO HOW MANY ARE IN OUR CLASS?

LARRY: *[He correctly counts the people represented on his paper, skipping the picture in the far left corner.]* Eleven.

TEACHER: IS THIS HOW MANY CHILDREN WE HAVE IN OUR CLASS?

LARRY: No. (He emits a loud sigh of exasperation.)

TEACHER: WHY NOT?

LARRY: Cause I said so. *[Pause.]* Because I didn't want too many.

TEACHER: ARE THESE PICTURES OF PEOPLE IN OUR CLASS? CAN YOU NAME THEM?

LARRY: Genie, Jafar, Aladdin, Abu, the bad guys and the magic carpet.

[For future reference, the teacher labels the figures as Larry identifies them.]

TEACHER: ARE THESE PEOPLE IN OUR CLASS?

LARRY: No, I'm making a puppet show.

Larry's teacher does not probe further. She is mindful of both the abilities and the limitations of kindergarten-aged children. Note that she pays attention to what Larry can do. She speaks to the importance of changing approaches, rather than expectations, when students don't complete a task as expected.

Teacher Reflection

Larry's representation helps me remember how young my students are. In his playful way he created his own piece of work. Did this come from a place of confusion, of underdeveloped thoughts, or from a place of playfulness and imagination? As we talked, I was struck by the fact that he knew this was not a picture representing the number of children in our class. I know that he knows there are twenty-one children. If I had asked him to snap together cubes in a tower he could have completed that task, though he might not have gotten the exact count, as he can skip or interchange some teen numbers. His comment about not wanting "too many" might be related to that difficulty, and then again, it might be that he tires of paper-and-pencil tasks. Working with Larry, I know that I need to vary the type of activity, but never lower my expectations.

I also was reminded that we recently attended a school assembly where we saw a puppet show of the story of Aladdin. Larry loved the performance and had been role-playing it in the dramatic play area for over a week. Was this just another extension of his play? Isn't this the important work of kindergartners?

Larry's representation may not have followed the directions of the set activity, but he certainly can represent his thoughts on paper.

The representation of data is a topic that requires attention at all grade levels throughout the school year. By the end of second grade, the National Council of Teachers of Mathematics recommends that students use counts, tallies, tables, bar graphs, and line plots to represent their data. Their representations should include labels and titles that clearly identify their work. "As students' questions become more sophisticated and their data sets larger, their use of traditional representations should increase" (NCTM 2000, 109).

The emphasis on students organizing and representing data sets themselves is a change from the years when children were shown ready-made representations and asked questions such as, "How many children chose red? Which color was chosen the most? How many fewer children chose yellow than green?" But can we assume that children who create their own displays can also interpret standard representations of data? The following episode from a second-grade classroom considers such a task.

How Many Nickels Do You Have?

One second-grade class had been working with money. Their teacher wanted to formulate a context to see how her students might use their new knowledge. Since it had been a few weeks since the class had participated in any new data experiences, she created the bar graph shown in Figure 5–17. Many graphical representations hung in the classroom from earlier whole-group experiences. On this day she wanted to see how students might individually interpret a bar graph that they didn't make, about a survey that they didn't take. She began with a brief whole-group

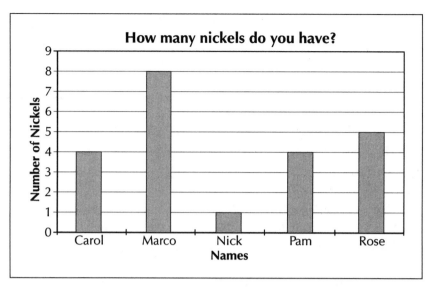

FIGURE 5–17 *Nickel graph*

discussion in order to give directions, help with any initial confusion, and establish expectations for the work.

TEACHER: TODAY WE'RE GOING TO LOOK CAREFULLY AT THIS GRAPH. *[She posts an enlarged copy for all to see.]* I HAVE A SMALL COPY OF THIS GRAPH FOR EACH OF YOU TO USE AT YOUR WORKSTATIONS. I'D LIKE YOU TO THINK ABOUT WHAT THE GRAPH TELLS YOU. YOU WILL HAVE A CHANCE TO DO SOME THINKING, DRAWING, AND WRITING ABOUT THE GRAPH. AFTER YOU HAVE HAD A CHANCE TO WORK ON YOUR OWN, THEN WE'LL SHARE OUR FINDINGS WITH EACH OTHER. FIRST, WHAT DO YOU NOTICE ABOUT THIS GRAPH?

JENNA: You can see all the names. Carol, Marco, Nick, Pam, Rose.

VLAD: How much? How high?

TEACHER: WHAT DO YOU MEAN?

VLAD: It means that there are a certain amount of blocks.

TEACHER: WHAT DO YOU MEAN BY BLOCKS?

HEIDI: There are little lines.

TOMMY: There's one big block per name, and you can figure out how high they are. Like how tall.

DOMINGO: Over here [pointing to the left-hand side of the graph], these numbers mean how much.

TEACHER: WHAT ELSE DO YOU NOTICE?

SERENA: It says, "How many nickels do you have?" It must be about nickels.

TEACHER: SERENA, IS THIS WHAT YOU ARE TALKING ABOUT? [Pointing to the question above the graph.]

SERENA: Yes. It's about nickels.

TEACHER: WHAT DOES SERENA MEAN BY THIS?

KAREN: Marco is the tallest.

DOMINGO: He has the most nickels.

TEACHER: I'D LIKE YOU TO GET STARTED WORKING ON YOUR OWN. WHAT DOES THE GRAPH TELL YOU? HOW DO YOU KNOW? IF YOU WERE TRYING TO EXPLAIN THE GRAPH TO SOMEBODY WHO HAD NEVER SEEN IT, WHAT WOULD YOU SAY? YOU WILL BE MAKING AN INTERPRETATION. DO YOU KNOW WHAT THAT MEANS?

GWEN: It's kind of like when you retell a story.

TEACHER: THAT'S A GOOD WAY TO THINK ABOUT IT. ARE YOU READY? YOU CAN DRAW OR WRITE TO TELL WHAT YOU LEARNED BY READING THIS GRAPH.

As the students move to their workspaces, the teacher begins to circulate around the room. Karen appears stuck. With a lot of prompting she says, "Marco is the tallest." This is the same statement that she expressed to the whole class.

TEACHER: WHAT DOES THE GRAPH TELL US?

KAREN: How tall they are [said in a questioning tone].

SALVADORE: [Sitting nearby.] It tells how much money.

FIONA: [Also at the same table.] No, it's how high.

SERENA: [The fourth child at this table.] It's the number of nickels.

KAREN: [Pointing to the column on her paper for Marco.] That's like Gina [another child in the class]. She's so tall.

TEACHER: IS HE REALLY THE TALLEST?

KAREN: Yes. It gives me a clue. Some kids are short and some are tall. Probably Nick is a baby. Marco has the tallest blocks.

TEACHER: IS THAT WHAT THIS GRAPH IS SHOWING?
KAREN: Yes, blocks.

Teacher Reflection

As I began to move around the classroom I was struck
by how seriously each child was taking this task.
Children who often are a bit restless when we settle in
to working independently during math seemed eager
to respond to the graph. Most children began by writing a type of narrative.

I noticed Karen right away. She had a confused look
about her. I also was thinking about her statement to
the group. I wondered if she really thought the graph
was about heights. We have graphed our heights, so this
makes sense, but I wonder what she thinks the purpose
of the question at the top of the page might be?

I tried to probe her thinking a bit, but didn't get very
far. Other children needed my attention so I moved
away. I don't like leaving a child who seems unsure,
but I also know I don't want to tell her too much. I
might confuse her more, or leave a false sense of
understanding. Giving her a little time to think on her
own, or maybe to interact with a peer, seemed right.
There certainly were some differences of opinion at her
table. Perhaps, I thought, they might talk this out
among themselves. I noticed that several children were
interchanging the ideas of measurement and height
with "most." It was time for me to move on.

Language plays a critical role in the development of ideas. It
is clear that some of the children are having trouble interpreting
the graph and are associating the different heights of the bars
with the heights of the children. Other students, however, seem
quite clear that the graph is about nickels. Even they, however,
often refer to heights rather than amounts. They seem to person-
ify the bars associated with each child.

Reviewing their written work, the teacher finds statements
such as, "It measures if you are taller or not. If you are taller you

get the most nickels." Such remarks clearly convey the confusion many children were having initially. They don't seem to grasp that it is the height of the bar, not the child, that is significant. In their group discussions, there was a constant interchange of the terms *tallest* and *most*. It is only after children focus on the printed question above the graph that they begin to correct this misperception. In the end, even Karen writes, "The chart shows how much nickels. The chart shows how many blocks there are." Though Karen does not add any more information to her interpretation, she does seem to grasp at least minimally, what the graph is about.

Many other children continue to link the terms *taller* and *more*, even though they understand the graph. Salvadore responds, "It measures who is taller. That means whoever is the tallest has the most nickels. Marco has the most nickels because he is the tallest." Salvadore's work (see Figure 5–18) shows that he re-creates the graph and then tries to order the "heights." When he speaks about his work, he is clear about the height issue. He says, "It's not really taller. It's just that Marco's line is taller." On the back of his paper, Salvadore calculates the total number of cents for each child. This work confirms that he sees

FIGURE 5–18   *Salvadore's work*

the relationship between the height of a bar on the graph and the number of nickels a particular child has.

The horizontal lines included on the graph get some of the children's attention. Mario writes, "Nick is touching the first line and Rose is touching the fifth line." Brooke writes, "Marco's measurement is up to 8. If you go to the top of Marco's measurement then to the left it says 8. So Marco has 8 nickels. Marco's 8 nickels equals 40 cents." She then redraws the graph, including the lines (see Figure 5–19). She does not include Marco in the

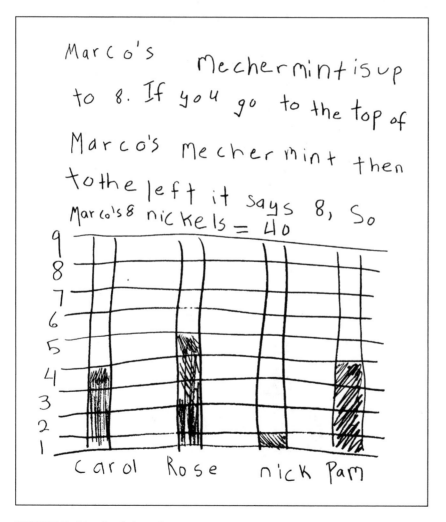

FIGURE 5–19   *Brooke's work*

graph. When her teacher asks about this, Brooke replies, "Oh, I wrote about him instead."

Several children write clear statements of facts. Heidi writes that Carol has four nickels, Marco has eight nickels, and so on through all five children depicted. Still other children add snippets of interpretation or summation. Jenna writes, "The numbers mean how many nickels." She records the number of nickels each child has and then adds, "Put them all together and you'll get twenty-two. Marco has the most money out of all because eight nickels equals forty."

The notion of a graph as a race or competition comes up often in conversation with young children. In this activity, it is not so much who is the winner but rather who is determined to have the most money. Whether referred to as the "tallest" or understood to be in possession of forty cents, Marco is the clear winner to these seven- and eight-year-olds. Gina's work (Figure 5–20), indicates the importance of comparisons within her own

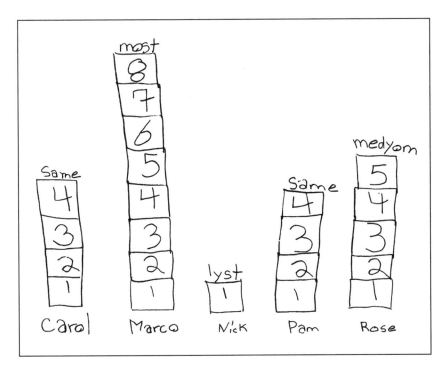

FIGURE 5–20 *Gina's work*

version of the graph. She numbers each box instead of using an axis and labels the columns *Same*, *Most*, *Least*, and *Medium*.

Lorenzo also begins with comparisons, using the terms *most* and *least*. He then adds, "Rose has one more nickel than Pam and Carol. Rose needs three more, and Pam and Carol need four more, and Nick needs seven more to have the same amount of nickels as Marco." On the back of his paper he identifies the children by their first initials and gives the value of the nickels that they have.

Claire creates a different type of representation (see Figure 5–21). She writes each child's name on her paper and then portrays the number of nickels they have using circled Ns. Since she completes this relatively quickly, her teacher asks her to write down some things she noticed about the graph. Claire makes twelve observations (see Figure 5–22).

Gwen's work (see Figure 5–23) shows the number of nickels for each child in the survey and the total number of nickels. She also adds a statement about the demographics: "There are five people. Three girls and two boys." She reports that there are twenty-two nickels, for a total of 120 cents. She discloses how she arrived at this incorrect amount during the whole-class debriefing session.

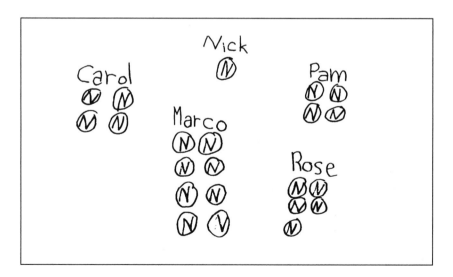

FIGURE 5–21   *Claire's representation*

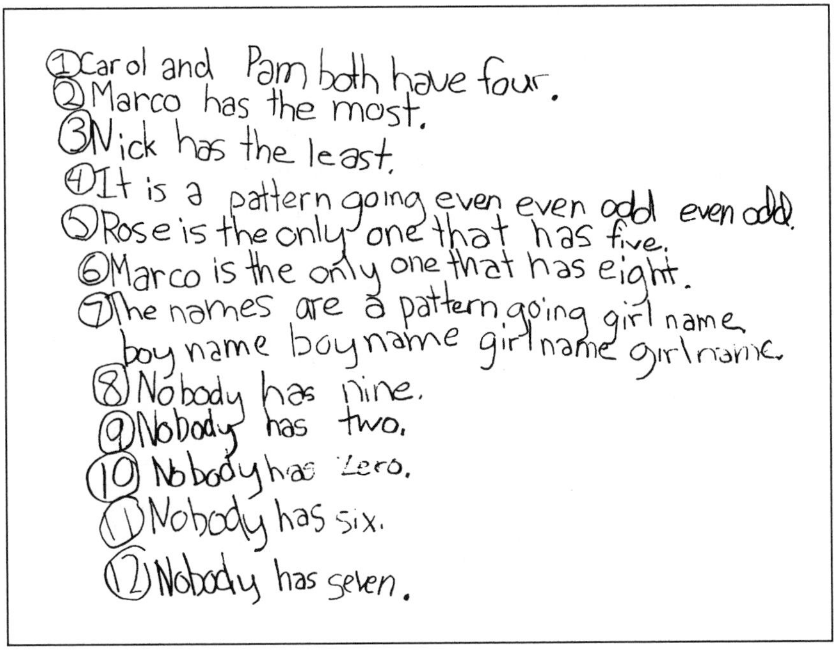

FIGURE 5-22   *Claire's twelve statements*

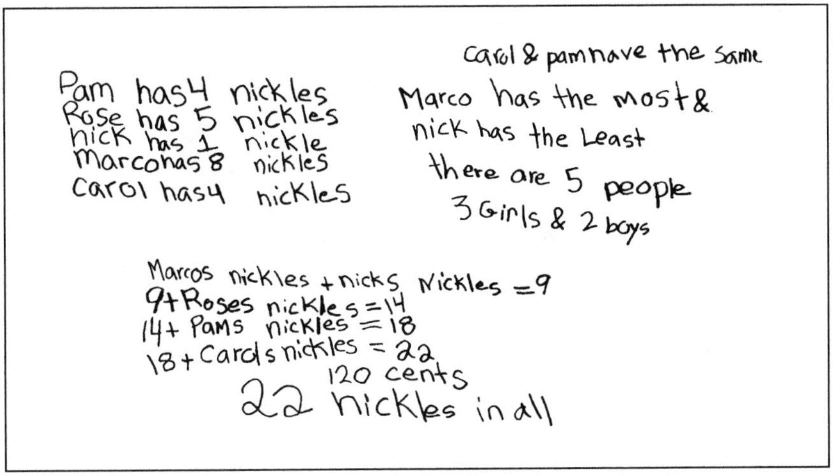

The image shows handwritten statements:

1. Carol and Pam both have four.
2. Marco has the most.
3. Nick has the least.
4. It is a pattern going even even odd even odd.
5. Rose is the only one that has five.
6. Marco is the only one that has eight.
7. The names are a pattern going girl name, boy name boy name girl name girl name.
8. Nobody has nine.
9. Nobody has two.
10. Nobody has zero.
11. Nobody has six.
12. Nobody has seven.

FIGURE 5-23   *Gwen's work*

The image shows handwritten work:

Pam has 4 nickles
Rose has 5 nickles
nick has 1 nickle
Marco has 8 nickles
Carol has 4 nickles

Carol & pam have the same
Marco has the most &
nick has the Least
there are 5 people
3 Girls & 2 boys

Marcos nickles + nicks Nickles = 9
9 + Roses nickles = 14
14 + Pams nickles = 18
18 + Carols nickles = 22
120 cents
22 nickles in all

TEACHER: WHAT IS THIS GRAPH ABOUT?

HEIDI: **Money.**

TEACHER: HOW DO YOU KNOW?

HEIDI: Because they have nickels.

TEACHER: HOW DO YOU KNOW THEY HAVE NICKELS?

TOMMY: The question says, "How many nickels?"

TEACHER: WITHOUT THAT QUESTION, WOULD WE HAVE KNOWN?

JENNA: On the side it says number of nickels.

LORENZO: Because it says number of people and how many nickels you have. First Marco has eight, Rose has five, Carol and Pam have four, and Nick has one. They can't be that tall.

TEACHER: A LOT OF PEOPLE WERE SAYING THAT MARCO WAS THE TALLEST. WHAT DOES THAT MEAN?

JENNA: Well, I sort of thought it meant that, but then I got that it meant that he had the most nickels.

LORENZO: It's not about how tall you are. It's about how tall the big blocks are.

TEACHER: IS THERE ANYTHING ELSE YOU LEARNED FROM THIS GRAPH?

DOMINGO: Are we going to go around and tell each other? Can each person say one thing?

LIONEL: Marco is touching the eighth line.

SCOTT: It matters if it's tall or not; if it's the tallest, you've got the most nickels.

DOMINGO: I noticed there's a very skinny line that goes across.

TEACHER: DOES THAT LINE HELP YOU?

SALVADORE: Because it tells you. The number means how many nickels they have. Like Carol has four. The line goes to that number.

DAVID: Marco's measurement is up to eight.

GWEN: There's one hundred twenty cents if you add all the nickels together.

TEACHER: HOW DO YOU KNOW THAT?

GWEN: I know there's twenty-two nickels. If I had ten nickels that's one hundred—no, ten is fifty—fifty plus fifty is one hundred, then two nickels, that would be another twenty. [Note the minor error here. If she had recognized two nickels as ten, her total amount would have been correct.] Five, four, that's nine; nine and five, that's fourteen; plus Pam's nickels, that's eighteen. Then eighteen plus Carol's four nickels makes twenty-two.

CLAIRE: Carol and Pam both have four nickels. The blocks both go to four.

SALVADORE: Marco has the most nickels.

TEACHER: WHO HAS THE LEAST AMOUNT?

CHORUS: Nick.

TEACHER: WHO HAS THE NEXT AMOUNT?

CHORUS: Pam and Carol.

SALVADORE: Then Rose, then Marco.

SERENA: Pam and Carol have the same amount of nickels.

Once again we see how discussion supports student learning. This teacher clearly believes in giving her students time to think and talk about their thinking, to struggle through confusing notions, and to share their work and conclusions.

While initially confusing to many students, as they talk about the graph they come to agree that it is about the number of nickels held by various individuals. The significance of the "little lines" continued to intrigue many children. The traditional graph helped them to see the importance of the left-hand axis.

Later the teacher wonders if the graph would have been easier for the children if she had used pictures of nickels rather than bars. She knows she will provide a similar experience within the next few days so that the children can build on what they have learned today. Maybe she'll provide Karen with a more concrete representation so that she can better make the connection. It's difficult to know what to do when trying something new, but this teacher believes strongly in providing children with challenges so that they can wrestle with important mathematical ideas. Data collection and representation offer many such challenges. As teachers, we just have to make sure that it is the students who are doing the work.

6

Investigating Geometry with Pictures and Words

Young children have a natural curiosity about the physical world. They are intuitively forming geometric ideas as they learn to navigate and describe their surroundings. They develop ways to solve problems when, for example, they run out of certain-shaped blocks or when their block structures fall down. Comments such as, "Let's rebuild it with the big ones on the bottom"; "I know, I can use two of these triangles to make a square"; "This goes over here so that it looks the same, only opposite"; and "Put it up behind where the pointy part is" demonstrate how block play helps to develop ideas about balance, symmetry, size, and shape. As children build, they form intuitive ideas about the relationships among two-dimensional and three-dimensional shapes. They become familiar with attributes of shapes and acquire a positional vocabulary. So how do our classrooms build on their rich experience and interest? How do we foster ways for children to communicate their geometric ideas?

Children enter kindergarten having already developed some ideas about shape. Many students can easily distinguish among circles, triangles, and squares. (This is not to infer that young children know that a square is a four-sided figure with four right angles and sides of equal length. They simply are able to recognize what a square looks like.) However, this early knowledge increases only minimally during their elementary and middle school years (Clements 2000).

We must provide our students with opportunities to learn a variety of geometric ideas. Our students' geometric descriptions and representations can provide us with important insight into their thinking. They can provide us with a platform on which we can extend their ideas. Consider the following example from a first-grade classroom.

What Do Children Know About Shapes?

It is January, and the teacher gathers the children together and tells them that they are about to begin a new unit, geometry. As she introduces this word, she shows it to them as written on chart paper. "Does anyone know what geometry is?" she asks. Most of the students shake their heads back and forth.

One child offers, "It's like finding places in the world. Like using a map."

"You may be thinking of geography," the teacher replies, and writes this word below the already recorded *geometry*. "Can anyone see something similar about these words?"

A few children recognize that both words begin with "geo" and share this insight with their classmates. The teacher explains that "geo" refers to the earth. She then inquires, "What else might we study about the earth or the physical world besides where things are on a map?" When one child replies, "shapes and stuff," the teacher asks, "What do you know about shapes?"

The children then take turns naming several two-dimensional geometric shapes. "You have named many shapes," the teacher comments. "I'd like you to draw and write what you know about shapes."

Most students draw two to four shapes and attempt to present one fact about each. Julie draws a circle, labels it as such, and asserts that this shape has zero points. She also draws a square, a triangle, and a rectangle. Again, she labels the shapes and identifies the number of "pons" (points). Note that the angles of her square and rectangle are ninety degrees (see Figure 6–1).

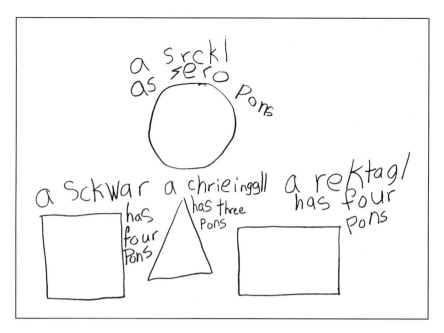

FIGURE 6–1　*Julie's work*

Because the children are familiar with pattern blocks, some of the students include a hexagon in their work. Maggie traces the bottom face of a hexagon piece from the pattern blocks set. She puts a finger on one of the vertices of her traced figure and begins to count the others. "One, two, three, four, five," she counts. "Hmm, I better do it again." This time she does not keep a finger stationary. She counts to seven as she recounts her initial vertex. Something compels her to count again. She places a finger just in front of one of the vertices and counts, "One, two, three, four, five, six; I *thought* there were six sides."

Nigel also gets a hexagon block. He places it next to his paper and tries to draw it. He makes a figure with several angles and then counts them. Finding eight in his figure, he records that a hexagon has eight points and draws an arrow to each one (see Figure 6–2).

John's representation is quite detailed and well organized for this grade level (see Figure 6–3). His invented spelling has been interpreted for ease of reading.

John's comments about the colors of diamonds and triangles are telling. Often, students infer mathematically irrelevant

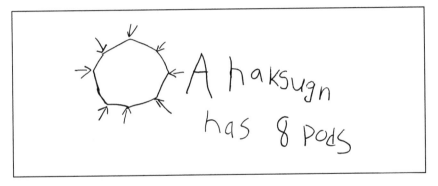

FIGURE 6–2   *Nigel's hexagon*

criteria from classroom materials. For example, triangular shapes represented in classrooms are almost exclusively isosceles or equilateral, with their base at the bottom. Rectangles are almost always depicted longer than they are wide. No wonder many children fail to recognize "tall and skinny" rectangles or scalene triangles. Perhaps examples of diamond shapes in John's classroom are limited to the pattern blocks. This is problematic for another reason as well. How will John learn that diamond is the *shape* of the top face of the block, not the block itself?

As a group, the students tend to identify one attribute about a shape, the number of sides or vertices (referred to as points or corners). John is one of only two students in the class who connect a shape to a real object. The other student, Agatha, writes, "It looks like a sun and a ball" underneath her drawing of a circle. Only two of the students relate one shape to another. Janet writes that an oval is "like a circle only longer." Marc describes a rectangle as a "stretched-out square."

Teacher Reflection

I am pleased with the students' responses. We have not done any formal work with geometry this year, yet the children know quite a bit. Some students are beginning to move beyond circles, squares, rectangles, and triangles with inclusion of ovals and hexagons. They are clearly interested in the number of sides or vertices. Although they are not always accurate and they don't

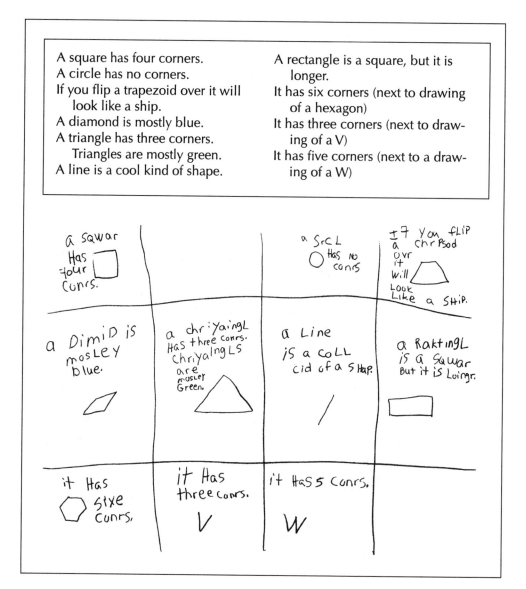

The box at the top of the figure contains:

A square has four corners.
A circle has no corners.
If you flip a trapezoid over it will look like a ship.
A diamond is mostly blue.
A triangle has three corners. Triangles are mostly green.
A line is a cool kind of shape.

A rectangle is a square, but it is longer.
It has six corners (next to drawing of a hexagon)
It has three corners (next to drawing of a V)
It has five corners (next to a drawing of a W)

FIGURE 6–3   *John's work*

use standard terminology, they have clearly observed that the name of a shape is related to the number of sides or vertices that it has.

It was amazing to watch Maggie repetitively count the vertices in her hexagon drawing until she got the expected "six." Confidence in her knowledge allowed her to reject "five" and "seven," yet she still needed to count to confirm her thinking. She talked about the number of sides, yet counted the vertices. Does she know that they will be the same or is her language causing her confusion?

I want to build on what these children know. I want to encourage them to describe, classify, compare, and represent shapes. I want to acknowledge their invented terms, but introduce the standard ones as well. I want to get a better sense of how their geometric ideas develop over time.

One way to gain a sense of how children's ideas develop over time is to examine how younger and older students respond to the same task. Pablo's work is fairly representative of the kindergarten children who are asked to draw and tell about the shapes they know. He draws a triangle, square, rectangle, and circle (see Figure 6–4), but not all of the angles in his square and rectangle appear to be ninety degrees. When his teacher asks about his shapes, he replies that a triangle has three sides and that a square and a rectangle have four sides. He does not mention the circle.

Janice makes the same shapes as Pablo. She tells her teacher, "The triangle has three points and the circle doesn't have

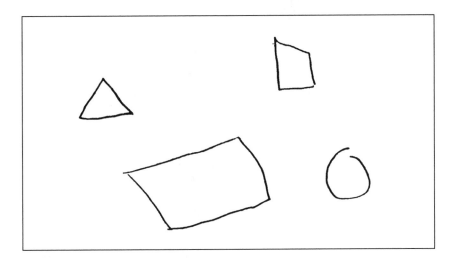

FIGURE 6–4   *Pablo's work*

any. It just goes round and round." She places her finger on the rectangle and describes it as being long and kind of wide. She then looks at the square and says, "This is like the rectangle, but a little shorter."

Another child, Becka, also mentions the similarities between a square and a rectangle. She points to her rectangle and says, "I think this might be a square too. It's the same thing, but it's longer."

The teacher, who wasn't aware that a square is also a rectangle until after teaching for several years, marvels at these children's intuitive sense of sameness. Too often, children lose this insight about rectangles and squares through school activities that aim at differentiating these shapes. This teacher wants to build on their correct intuition. "Yes, squares and rectangles are very much alike," she says. "In fact, we could call this shape [pointing to the square] a square rectangle."

Many of the kindergarten drawings include hearts and stars. (Only a few first graders included these shapes.) Conchita draws several shapes (see Figure 6–5). She describes her circle as "having

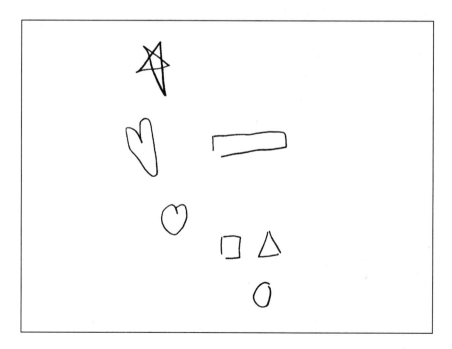

FIGURE 6–5   *Conchita's work*

no corners," and then gives the correct number of corners for the triangle, square, and rectangle. Next she directs her teacher's attention to the heart, describing it as "two lumps and a point." Lastly, she puts her finger on the star and says, "It's up in the sky."

Not all of the kindergarten children refer to the geometric features of their shapes. Misty (see Figure 6–6) points to the star she has made and tells her teacher, "I like them." She includes a pumpkin in her drawing and says, "I love pumpkins." For her hearts she adds, "They're actually pretty." Finally she points to the triangle and observes simply, "I drew it."

A few kindergarten children attempt to draw polygons other than triangles, squares, rectangles, and circles. Three children include well-formed ovals, described as "long circles." Jake's drawing includes an attempt at a diamond (see Figure 6–7). He tells his teacher, "A diamond has two corners. One on one end and then the other."

After drawing a rectangle, square, triangle, and circle, Marietta draws another circle and then makes six lines around it (see Figure 6–8). "When I add the lines," she announces, "it makes an octa-

FIGURE 6–6 *Misty's work*

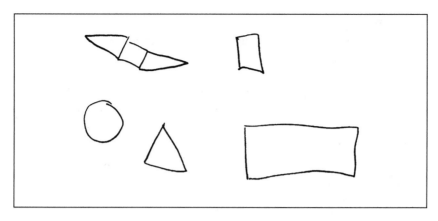

FIGURE 6–7   *Jake's work*

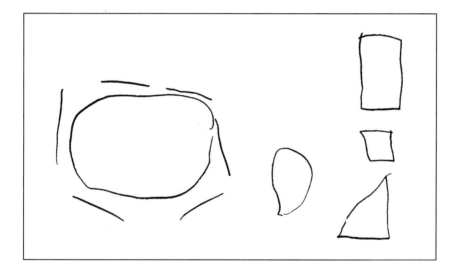

FIGURE 6–8   *Marietta's work*

gon." She confuses the names octagon and hexagon, but was clearly attempting great complexity in her representation.

The second-grade students' work demonstrates a greater variety over that of earlier years. Eddie creates a person using a variety of shapes (see Figure 6–9). As expected, he differentiates in his count between the squares and the rectangles. Although he draws a triangle in a nontraditional orientation (the nose), he refers to it as an "upside-down triangle." In his drawing at the

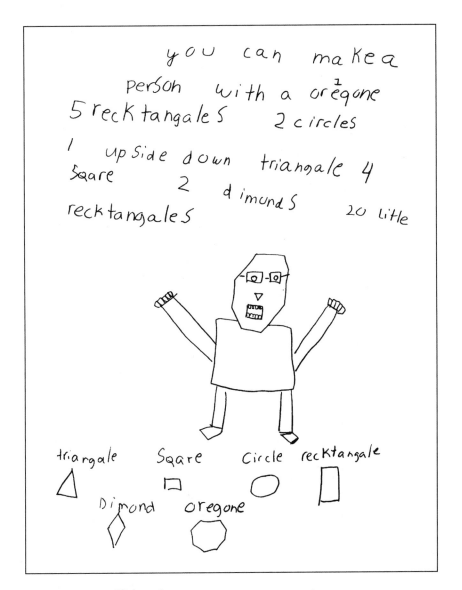

you can make a
person with a oregone[1]
5 reck tangales   2 circles
1 upside down triangale 4
Sqare
        2   dimunds
reck tangales   20 litle

triangale   Sqare   Circle   recktangale

Dimond   oregone

FIGURE 6-9   Eddie's work

bottom of the page, the triangle is depicted in the traditional position.

It is usually not until this grade level that children begin to identify "corners" and "lines" as two separate entities. Marybeth's work (Figure 6-10) indicates several different attributes of shapes. She refers to the lengths as well as the number of sides.

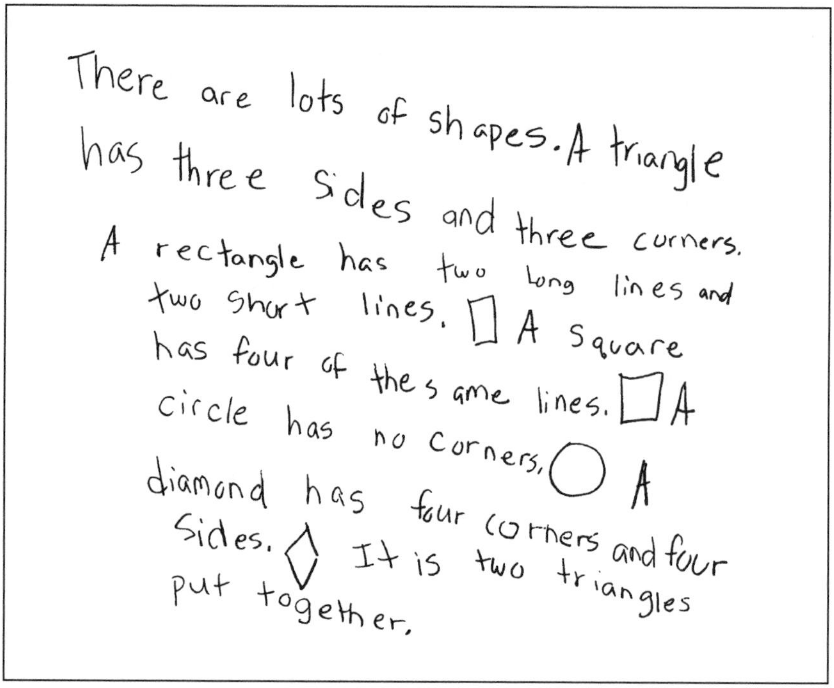

There are lots of shapes. A triangle has three sides and three corners. A rectangle has two long lines and two short lines. ☐ A square has four of the same lines. ☐ A circle has no corners, ◯ A diamond has four corners and four sides. ◇ It is two triangles put together.

FIGURE 6–10   *Marybeth's work*

She also notes that two triangles can be put together to make a diamond.

Several of the children refer to three-dimensional figures. Jackie shows a cube and a rectangular prism, yet labels them *square* and *rectangle*. He does write *cube* in parenthesis beneath his label *square*, but notes that the form has only four corners (see Figure 6–11).

Mac draws two squares, one behind and just to the right of the other. As he connects the two squares to make a cube, he announces, "This is so cool. I learned this in art." On his recording he writes, "I know how to draw a square in 3-D."

Lyle also includes a cube in his drawings, labeling it *box*. Ben draws a cube and a rectangular prism. Like Jackie, he refers to these shapes as a square and a rectangle. However, he identifies them as having six sides. Nikki's work is noteworthy as she "unfolds" her cube into a two-dimensional shape made up of six squares (see Figure 6–12).

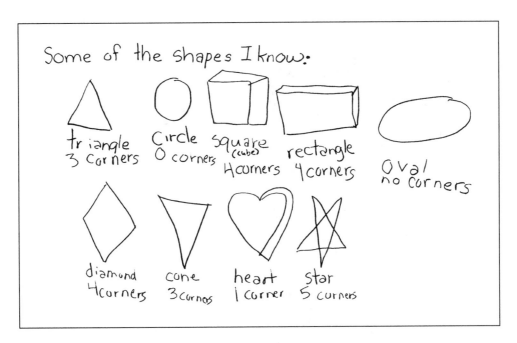

Some of the shapes I know:

triangle
3 corners

Circle
0 corners

square
(cube)
4 corners

rectangle
4 corners

oval
no corners

diamond
4 corners

cone
3 corners

heart
1 corner

star
5 corners

FIGURE 6–11 *Jackie's work*

These children frequently make connections to real-world objects. Missy notes that ovals are shaped like eggs. Nancy states, "If you cut the circle in half it will look like a cave, and if you cut the cave in half it will look like a pizza." Sal's depiction shows that a square is like a computer screen, a circle like a clock, and a rectangle like a piece of paper. Matthew makes several pictures of real-world objects (see Figure 6–13 on page 137). Note that although he recognizes the yield sign as triangular, in his drawing, he has shown it in the traditional position.

It is clear that this "shape work" changes over the grade levels. The amount of writing increases and is more skillful. The ability of the children to draw the figures improves. As the older children become familiar with different aspects of shape, there is more variety in their representations. It is this variety, however, that leads to nagging questions. Is the variation in older students' work attributable to their varied interests and experiences outside of school? Would there be more similarity if more formal learning were provided? How will students be able to recognize a nonregular six-sided polygon as a hexagon if we never provide

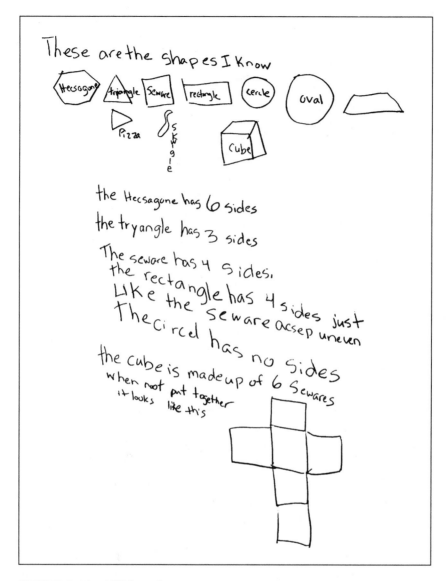

FIGURE 6–12   *Nikki's work*

them opportunities to consider one? Are they only learning connections between two- and three-dimensional shapes in art class?

What About Three-Dimensional Figures?

Consider the form shown in Figure 6–14. If you were looking at actual blocks rather than this representation, do you think that

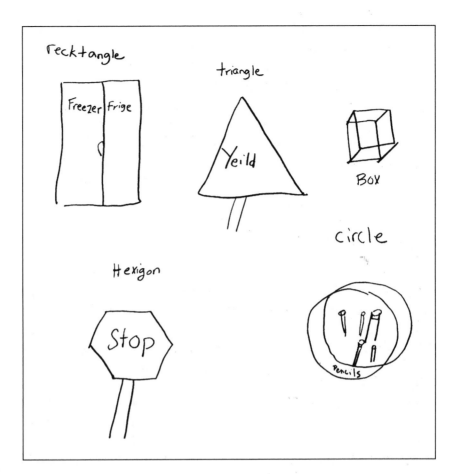

FIGURE 6–13   *Matthew's work*

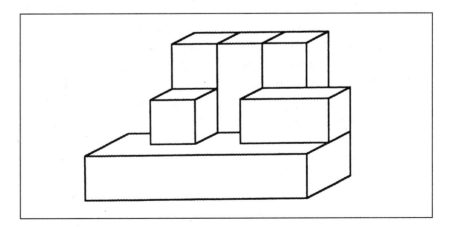

FIGURE 6–14   *Three-dimensional drawing*

you could draw them? Can you imagine what this configuration would look like if it were tipped so that the back face became the bottom and then the entire figure were rotated to face you? Many elementary school teachers do not have confidence in their ability to depict a three-dimensional design and to visualize such figures being rotated in space. A sense of their own deficits or insecurities often leads to a lack of attention to work with three-dimensional figures in their classrooms. As a result, some children never have a chance to work with three-dimensional figures in school other than at the block area in kindergarten. Further, many kindergarten classrooms regard this activity as play, and rarely afford children the opportunity to formally discuss the geometric ideas gleaned from this play.

Some educators argue that this lack of attention to three-dimensional figures in the classroom results in differences between the mathematical abilities of males and females. Gender differences in mathematics vary across grade levels and skills. Studies in this area are complex, and sometimes contradictory. For many years, however, research on the ability to mentally rotate three-dimensional figures has consistently favored males (Casey, Nuttall, and Pezaris 2001). Many believe that the types of activities children engage in outside of school contribute to this difference. Many girls have fewer spatial experiences compared with boys. If girls are to reach their potential, classrooms must give specific attention to the development of spatial thinking, particularly with three-dimensional figures.

One way students can learn more about three-dimensional figures is to represent them in a drawing. While some children may be more adept than others at depicting three-dimensional figures, the act of drawing encourages a focus on the characteristics of these forms. When children carefully observe and describe three-dimensional figures, similarities and differences begin to be noted. As students share their drawings and begin to experiment with each other's techniques, their representation skills become more proficient.

It is late fall when a second-grade teacher asks her students to draw and write about three-dimensional figures. She places one, two, or three Geoblocks in paper bags. Each of the bags is labeled so that she can identify the individual collections. The students are instructed to choose a bag, draw the blocks that are inside, and tell what they notice about the blocks. Each student is then asked to repeat the activity, using a different collection, making sure that at least one of the bags chosen contains two or three blocks.

Massie first chooses a bag with a triangular prism. She takes the block out of the bag and rotates it so that she can examine it from different perspectives. She places it on the table so that a triangular face is turned toward her with the longest side of the triangle at the bottom. She stares at the block for a bit and then draws it (see Figure 6–15). After her drawing is finished, she picks the block up again. She counts both the faces and the vertices. Then she places the block back on the table exactly as it

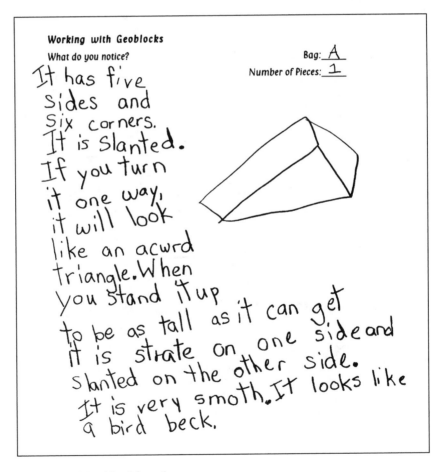

Working with Geoblocks

What do you notice?

Bag: A
Number of Pieces: 1

It has five Sides and Six corners. It is Slanted. If you turn it one way, it will look like an acwrd triangle. When you stand it up to be as tall as it can get It is strate on one side and Slanted on the other side. It is very smoth. It looks like a bird beck.

FIGURE 6–15 *Massie's work*

was, but upside down. She tries to balance it and finds that it falls down each time. (Note her written reference to the "awkward triangle.") Next, she places the block on the table with the triangular face toward her, but this time, the shortest edge is at the bottom. She runs her finger along the slanted rectangular face. She then writes about what she has noticed.

Leslie chooses a bag containing three blocks. She first takes out the rectangular prism. She counts the vertices and faces and records what she observes. Next she draws the figure. When finished, she marks a line across her page (see Figure 6–16). She

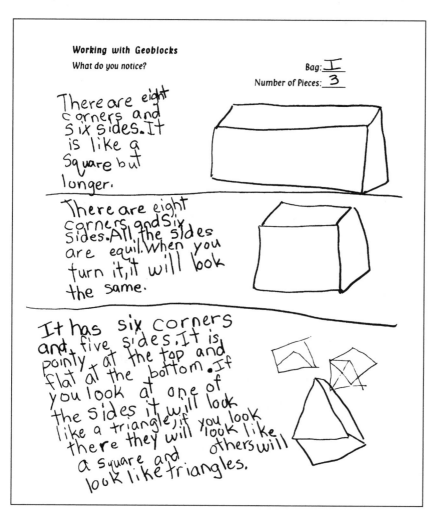

Working with Geoblocks
What do you notice?

Bag: I
Number of Pieces: 3

There are eight corners and six sides. It is like a square but longer.

There are eight corners and six sides. All the sides are equil. When you turn it, it will look the same.

It has six corners and five sides. It is pointy at the top and flat at the bottom. If you look at one of the sides it will look like a triangle. if you look there they will look like a square and others will look like triangles.

FIGURE 6–16 *Leslie's work*

then takes a cube from the bag and looks at it carefully as she rotates it in her hand. She counts the vertices and faces. She writes and draws about this block and marks another line across her page.

Finally, Leslie takes a triangular prism from the bag. Once again she rotates the figure and does some counting. When she finishes writing her observations, she looks carefully at the block again. As is clear from her representation, this piece is the most difficult for her to draw. She is dissatisfied with her first two attempts and erases them. She sighs deeply and says, "This one is very hard."

"What makes it hard?" her teacher asks.

"It's not like the others. It's all slanty-like. I don't know how to show that." Her teacher asks what she'd like to do. "I guess I could just show some of the sides," Leslie replies, and returns to her drawing. Upon finishing, she turns to a friend sitting beside her and displays her drawing and the collection of Geoblocks. "Do you know which of these blocks this one is?" she asks, pointing to her representation of the prism. Leslie beams when her friend chooses the correct block.

Peter's bag contains two triangular prisms. He takes out both blocks and places them on his desk, trying several different orientations. "I can't make them look alike," he announces. He then counts the number of faces for each figure. He asks a classmate if he can borrow her "ramp" and counts the faces on that piece as well. He then begins to write and draw (see Figure 6–17). His teacher asks him which block is shown in his first diagram.

"Neither," he replies. "It's just a ramp. Turns out they all have five, even if they're different."

Jenny's, Russ's, and Kent's recordings illustrate their emerging abilities. Their drawings are representative of the ways in which several children at this grade level first try to show three-dimensional figures. Note that none of these children writes about the characteristics of their blocks.

Jenny's bag contains a large and a small cube. She places the small cube on top of the larger one. She draws one face of each block. Then she places the small cube on top of the large cube and draws the outline of the shape they form together (see Figure 6–18).

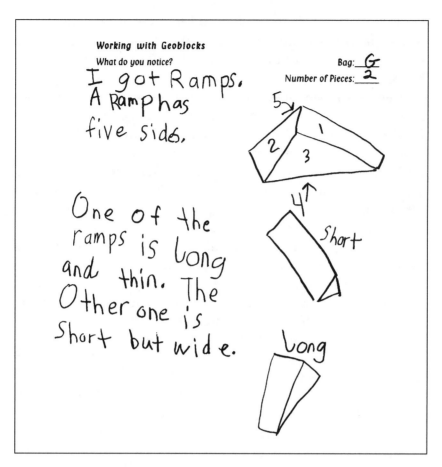

Working with Geoblocks

What do you notice?

Bag: __G__
Number of Pieces: __2__

I got Ramps.
A Ramp has
five sides.

One of the
ramps is long
and thin. The
Other one is
short but wide.

5

2
1
3

4↑
Short

Long

FIGURE 6–17   *Peter's work*

Russ begins as many children do, by tracing one face of his rectangular prism. For some children, tracing provides a way to begin the process. This works particularly well for students who realize that they do not need to show all faces (just those that they can actually see) and who are willing to draw in a more freehand manner once that first face is depicted. For some children, however, tracing can actually make the task more complicated. This is particularly true if they trace each face and then have to determine how to show the faces in relationship to one another. In his representation, Russ wants to include all of the faces (see Figure 6–19). While he doesn't connect the faces, he does demonstrate the understanding that some of the faces are

FIGURE 6–18   *Jenny's work*

identical. Russ records a 2 in the rectangles to indicate pairs of matching faces on the block.

Kent's bag contains a cube, a rectangular prism, and a triangular prism. For each shape, he picks up the block and begins by tracing the face that he sees directly. Then, as can be seen in Figure 6–20 on page 145, he draws (freehand) each of the adjacent faces as if they were facing toward him as well.

Like Kent's, Joe's drawing includes no written observations. His representation, however, is quite sophisticated (see Figure 6–21 on page 146). He shows his two blocks in three different configurations, and is one of only three students to use shading to suggest depth. Note that in his first and third drawings, he first shows each block in its entirety and then erases the portion of

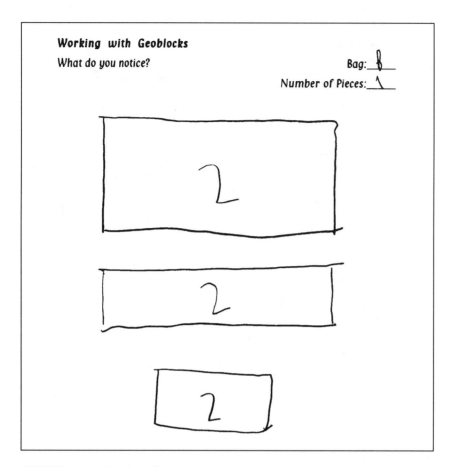

Working with Geoblocks
What do you notice? Bag:
Number of Pieces:

FIGURE 6–19 *Russ's work*

the prism that is behind the other block. He is the only child to represent the blocks in a front/back relationship.

Alice and Jason begin by drawing each of their three blocks separately. Then they combine the blocks in a second drawing. Alice puts the pieces together to form a bridge (Figure 6–22, page 147). Jason offers two arrangements of his blocks suggesting real-world objects (Figure 6–23, page 148).

Teacher Reflection

As I observed my students tackling this task, I couldn't help but watch their bodies weave and bob as they

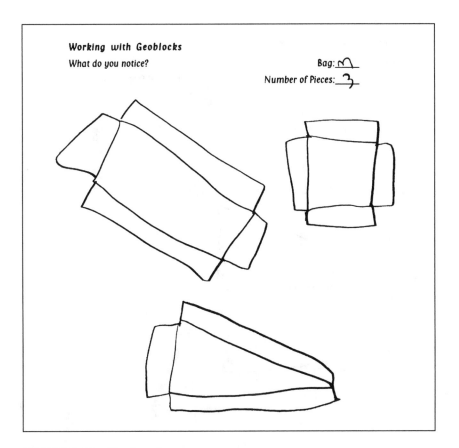

FIGURE 6–20   *Kent's work*

rotated a block in their hand or tried looking at one or two blocks from different angles. I also noticed that many children said more about the relationship between the blocks than they wrote or drew. I heard comments such as: "I have two cubes. One is double the other. I think this is called a rectangle because it has rectangles on the sides. I can count the lines, corners and the spaces."

As the work session went along, I noticed students comparing ideas and also playing with the blocks. They would arrange the blocks as though they were building and match faces as they did so. I saw children smile when faces were congruent and continue to flip

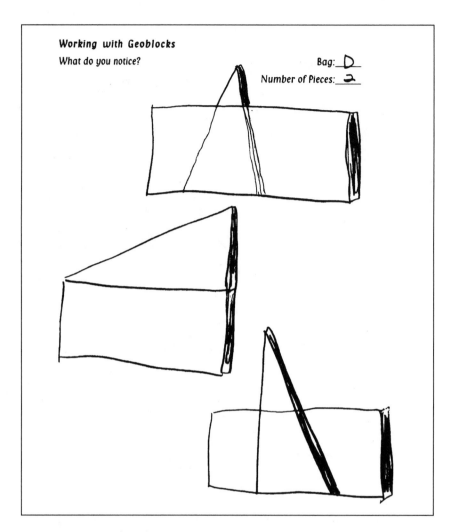

FIGURE 6-21   *Joe's work*

and turn pieces if dissatisfied by the configuration. They looked like artists and engineers.

I had asked the class to pay particular attention to putting the blocks back in the proper bag. They really took this task seriously; I even heard one group argue as to which "triangle" (triangular prism) went in which bag. It turns out that they had identical blocks, but they wanted to make sure the "right" one got back in each bag. Were the children so focused on the task of

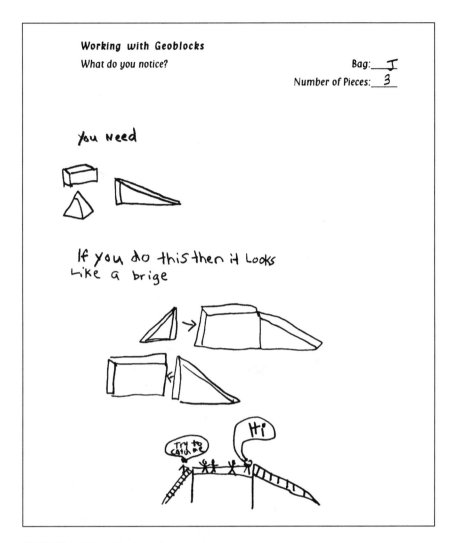

FIGURE 6–22 *Alice's work*

describing and representing each of the blocks, that they had a hard time pulling back and seeing the bigger picture? After all, if the blocks were identical, did it matter?

I plan to have my students share their work along with what they were thinking about as they made their recordings. I want them to talk about the different techniques they used when representing the shapes

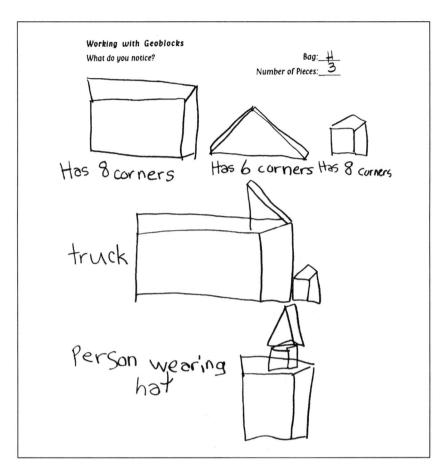

FIGURE 6–23 *Jason's work*

and to focus more on geometric concepts and vocabulary. It is not always easy to recall what to name these blocks. I noticed that most, if not all, of the children relied on two-dimensional language.

When planning, I wondered if my students would be intimidated by trying to capture all of their ideas on paper. I suspected that this activity would be a stretch for them, and knew that I shied away from such drawing tasks. I wanted to push all of us. Thinking about the composition of shapes/objects is important. Being able to decompose each shape/object so that one can see and describe relationships between 2-D and 3-D figures is also critical. Working with Geoblocks, my students can hone their visual perception skills, as well as learn to be both more precise and more flexible in their thinking.

I was pleased with how things went. I was excited to see the combination of writing and drawing, to listen to their conversations. I wonder if I could have done this activity when I was in second grade.

How Can Pictures Help?

So far we have examined how the representation of geometric figures can both stimulate the development of ideas and provide teachers with a window into students' thinking. Asking students to share and describe their representations can clarify ideas and stimulate the use of vocabulary related to shape and position.

Verbally conveying information can be difficult for all of us. We might use the wrong words, or explain things in the wrong order, or forget to take into account the perspectives of others. Consider these two everyday examples.

When trying to identify a pair of earrings in a display case, a shopper describes the pair as being to the right of the large hoops. The clerk looks to the right from her perspective and initially identifies the wrong earrings. "No, the other right," the shopper proclaims.

A five-year-old is walking in a mall with her family and becomes intrigued by a shiny new car on display. She motions that she wants to look at it. Getting no response she points and says, "Over here," as she pulls away from the person who is holding her hand. The family spends a few moments looking at the automobile and then moves on. Later the child is looking over a railing from the upper level of the mall and spots the same car. "You can see it from *down* here, too!" she explains with surprise.

It is common for young children to point in the direction of what they want or are trying to describe. Gradually, through natural conversations and everyday situations, vocabulary for describing what objects look like and where they are located in relationship to other things is developed. Yet words sometimes get confused and multiple perspectives are not always considered. Ample opportunities to converse with others are needed in order to develop expressive and receptive language that is both precise and easily understood.

In mid-winter, a kindergarten teacher reflects on her observations of children trying to describe to a classmate an object of interest in the block area, dramatic play area, or art center. She thinks about how they sometimes struggle and quickly revert to pointing to the object or getting it themselves. She thinks about how they move blocks on their own when they can't get a classmate to follow their directions.

The teacher decides to create an activity that will require students to work with vocabulary related to shape and position. She remembers the collage-like pictures in the book *The Shape of Things*, by Dayle Ann Dodds. Such illustrations help children see that shapes are all around us. But this teacher wants her students to grapple with positional vocabulary as well. The school's art teacher is also interested in this idea, and agrees to create a picture to stimulate conversation.

Figure 6–24 is the art teacher's rendition of a parade scene. The children are immediately interested when their teacher displays the picture and asks, "What do you see?" As they begin to

FIGURE 6–24   *Parade scene*

talk about the illustration their conversation moves back and forth between labeling the objects shown—fire engine, ladder, dog, clown, balloons—and naming the shapes that they easily recognize, such as circle, rectangle, and triangle. It is important that students recognize geometric figures in their world. Also, noticing the shapes of everyday objects can help children to more fluently draw and create designs and images on their own. The conversation is animated.

TINA: Balloons!

LOUIE: A dog.

ALYSSA: The sign on the airplane.

NATHAN: The fire engine has wheels. They're circles. There are triangles inside the wheels.

RASHID: It's a parade.

NADIA: I see a ladder and an alarm. The ladder is two thin and long rectangles and a few short ones across. [*As Nadia uses the word* across, *she moves her finger vertically in the air and motions up and down a few times. At the same time, she moves her head from left to right as though tracing the lines that make the rungs of the ladder.*]

TIMMY: Up there is a plane holding a flag with words on it.

TEACHER: WHERE IS THE PLANE?

TIMMY: Uphill, in the air.

Timmy begins to move toward the picture, but his teacher motions for him to wait. The impulse to use gestures in order to communicate precisely is keen in this exchange of kindergartners. But for now, Timmy's teacher wants the children to try to use their words.

TEACHER: WHERE IS THE BANNER?

MANUELLA: It's in the back of the plane.

BEVERLY: No, it's behind the plane.

NATHAN: That's the same thing.

BEVERLY: No, it's not.

MANUELLA: Yes, it is.

BEVERLY: In the back isn't behind. The flag is behind the plane because it is pulled. It's not in the back of the plane.

Behind; in the back—these words spark such clear images for some children but are remote for others. While Beverly is heated in her debate, most of her classmates appear unaffected and ready to move on. Hands are waving, signaling more responses.

JAMES: The clown has balloons.

ALYSSA: There are six [*motions her finger as though counting from her seat*], no seven, balloons in his hand.

NADIA: They are in the air.

CALEB: I see a dog.

TEACHER: WHERE IS THE DOG?

CALEB: Near the clown. It's on the road.

KYRA: It has clothes on.

NATHAN: He's up. His feet are up.

JAMES: He's walking.

KYRA: He's barking at the clown.

TEACHER: WHAT ELSE CAN YOU TELL ABOUT WHERE THE DOG IS?

ALYSSA: He's in back.

LOUIE: He's in the middle of the parade.

BEVERLY: He's in the middle of the clown and the fire engine.

VERA: He's going the wrong way.

ALYSSA: He wants to see more of the parade faster. He's going the other way!

In order to declare that the dog is going the "wrong way," Vera must have determined that the "right" way is the direction in which the fire engine and clown are headed. Louie identifies that the dog is in the middle of the parade, and Beverly adds that the dog is in the middle of the clown and the fire engine. Did she mean "in between"? The subtle and multiple meanings of such terms make it essential that children have opportunities to develop their positional language.

As the conversation continues, the children are able to speak with more sophistication and confidence about the picture.

LOUIE: The propeller in the front of the plane is like an X.

NADIA: There is a circle in the center of the propeller.

BEVERLY: The flag that the plane is pulling is a rectangle.

ALYSSA: It's kind of like a rectangle, but it's curvy.

TINA: I see ten rectangles on the ladder.

REBA: I see ten, too. There are ten little black rectangles but nine gray ones inside the ladder. The two on the end don't count because they don't have lines.

CALEB: Oh yeah, on the ends there aren't black things, so it is nine rectangles. Nine gray rectangles and ten black ones, plus two really long ones, one on the top and one on the bottom.

NATHAN: The wheels on the fire engine are funny. One has a triangle and the other kind of does.

BEVERLY: They are arrows; one points up. *[She extends her index finger and points up.]* The other is pointing this way. *[Beverly points her finger to the left.]*

TEACHER: WHICH WAY ARE THEY POINTING?

KYRA: One is a triangle. The other is an arrow.

JAMIE: One goes up and the other goes to the side *[using similar motions as Beverly]*.

Conversations about curvy rectangles and triangles that are sometimes a triangle and sometimes an arrow let us peek at shape and position through the eyes of young children. The idea that one wheel has rotated and thus the triangle is in a different position is intriguing to them, but causes confusion. The children try to make sense of this situation by calling the triangle an arrow. Once again, we see how children fail to recognize shapes shown in different positions as the same. How can we help our students to generalize about the characteristics of shapes in appropriate ways?

What About Using Technology?

Utilizing the technology available to us in today's world gives students opportunities to play with shape and position in new ways. Software that allows children to flip, turn, and slide shapes helps them to recognize shapes in different positions as well as to imagine shapes being manipulated in space. As a kindergartner selects a triangle from the tool bar, copies it, and then rotates it ninety degrees to the left, she sees the same configuration as the wheel of the fire engine.

Some programs allow users to shrink and expand shapes or to change their angles. Even simple drawing programs let us show basic shapes in a great variety of ways. Perhaps with exposure to such programs, students' confusions, underdeveloped ideas, and overgeneralizations about shape and their relative positions can be better addressed.

The use of software aids in the development of visual perception as well as dexterity. For children who find drawing or replicating their work on paper tedious, programs such as *Shapes—Making Shapes* (Clements and Meredith 1998) offer students the chance to show their ideas in a less cumbersome way. Further, unlike manipulation of concrete materials, these programs let children save their work, making it possible to retrieve and replay sequences of actions with the shapes.

Geometry has not received much attention in primary classrooms, yet it is integral to the study of mathematics. Geometric ideas permeate our world and provide different ways to solve problems. The exploration of geometry can provide students who struggle in other areas of mathematics with opportunities to shine. Early exposure to geometric ideas may help to lessen gender differences in spatial reasoning.

For children to develop their geometric thinking, they must have time to show and tell about their ideas. Providing a wide variety of materials for students to explore is also vital. Utilizing technology is just one more way we can differentiate instruction and offer new pathways to geometric learning.

7

Exploring the Sights and Sounds of Measurement

Young children gravitate to the measurement of objects in much the same way as they naturally build and ask questions about shapes in the world around them. Their interest in ideas of comparison is evident from a very young age. "Mine is longer" or "How come he got the bigger piece?" are the kind of comments heard long before children enter school. It is important that early-childhood classrooms capitalize on children's genuine interest in this area.

Solomon and Clayton are exploring with Unifix cubes. "Let's snap them *all* together," says Solomon.

Clayton replies, "Yeah, let's see how far we can make them go."

As these two kindergarten students begin to snap sets of cubes together, Maureen and Carolyn approach. "What are you doing? Can we help?" they ask.

Before long many of their classmates are busily snapping Unifix cubes together as well. The squeals of glee as the number of cubes in the bucket diminishes and the "train" becomes increasingly longer, tell much about this common, self-initiated, cooperative activity.

CLAYTON: I don't think we can use all of them.

SOLOMON: Yes, we can.

CLAYTON: Let's make them go under the table.

MAUREEN: We can stretch them around the room.

MIKEL: If we work together, we can do it.

LENA: Make sure we use all of the cubes.

RHEA: I'll check to make sure they're all together. *[As the children progress, some of the cubes snapped together earlier have come apart.]*

A few months later, another group of children is making a train of connected cubes. "Can we make it as long as me?" asks Tim.

"Lie down [pointing to the floor next to the train] and let's see," suggests Carrie.

Tim lies down next to the train and the children add each cube with new anticipation. "I think this will make it," announces Suzi as she attaches one more cube.

"Check me. Check me," demands Rachel and quickly lies down on the other side of the train, about a foot after the train begins.

"You're bigger," decides Robi, who begins to add some more cubes.

Teacher Reflection

So often I have seen my students empty every Unifix cube on the floor and then witnessed their tireless efforts to snap them together. This activity seems to have endless appeal. The children sometimes line up teddy bear counters or the hexagon pieces from the pattern block set in a similar manner, but nothing seems to intrigue them as much as linking these cubes. It's as if the children have an instinctual need to connect all of the cubes together or to make a train that reaches to some far-off point in the classroom.

What compels these children to see how far the train will stretch or to ensure that all of the cubes are attached? Am I observing a naturalistic need to measure our world? What is it about this activity that makes them so eager to cooperate? Whatever the motivation, it is clear that young children are fascinated by this activity. Over time, some begin to count the cubes as well, but at first, it is the sheer length of the train that draws their attention.

In the beginning of the year, their focus is simply on making long trains, to use all of the cubes. Next, they wonder if they can reach a specific location in the classroom. In my experience, it is later in the year when they begin to lie down next to the trains and compare them to the lengths of their bodies. They aren't particular about exactness. In fact, it takes them quite a while to see the need for a common starting point in order to make a more accurate comparison.

Determining which object is bigger or longer (smaller or shorter) is an important exploration. I want to help my students begin to think about precision as they continue to formulate ideas about comparison. I want to help them to talk about their ideas and to represent them in an organized way.

A Scientific Study

Observing a plant as it grows and develops through identified stages is a common exploration in early-childhood classrooms. In one kindergarten class, a study of an amaryllis has been conducted for several years. The teacher wants her students to think like scientists, to observe and describe what they see and to record changes over time. She has created observation sheets for her young scientists. The children are asked to observe the plant in different stages and to draw or write about what they notice. As the plant changes from a bulb to having a sprout and then buds, the children record these changes in their logs, making sure to date their observations (a stamp is used) and to compare their ideas with those of their classmates. For the past few years, the teacher has incorporated nonstandard measurement in the process.

To begin, the teacher gathers the children in the meeting area and presents them with an amaryllis bulb on a tray. "What do you think this is?" she queries. The children take turns picking up the bulb and turning it over in their hands. Once they've had time to examine the object, they begin to make predictions.

ALAN: I think it is an onion. I don't want to touch it. It will make me cry.

MAKEITHA: I don't think you eat this. Yuck. It looks like an onion, but it isn't.

SIDDARTH: I think these are strings [*drawing his finger along the roots of the bulb*].

HAROLD: No, I think those are roots.

PATSY: Yup, I think we can plant this. This is the bottom [*pointing to the roots*] and this is the top [*pointing to the opposite end while holding the bulb upright*].

KYLE: I agree with Alan. I know it's an onion.

CHERI: It's an onion.

PHIL: I hate onions.

Other children aren't convinced, but identifying the mystery object as an onion appears to be the most compelling idea. The children's next comments focus on the size of the object.

PHIL: This is bigger than a baseball.

ROCKY: It's smaller than a basketball.

CORRINE: A basketball is way too big. I can hold this in my hand [*placing the bulb in the palm of her hand*]. I can't hold a basketball this way.

JOY: It's still pretty big though.

The conversation is animated and the children become more and more anxious to find out what the object really is. The teacher decides it is time to tell them. "This is a bulb for a flower," she announces. "I agree, it looks like an onion. An onion is a part of a plant that grows underground. In this sense, it is a bulb, but one that we can eat. What else do you notice about this flower bulb?"

The children share observations about the "strings," which they learn are the roots. Harold and Patsy boast that their predictions were correct. The teacher draws the children's attention to the part of the bulb where the green shoot will grow. Then she reads the book *A Flower Grows* by Ken Robbins.

The children are delighted to see a picture of their mystery object in the book. They learn that this is a bulb for an amaryllis plant and that it will take several weeks before it begins to show any growth. Next, the children are given their initial recording sheets on which they are to draw a picture of the bulb. They make their representations, write their names, and stamp the date on their sheets, placing them in individual folders known as their "plant logs."

Finally, the bulb is planted. In order to help the children think about the number of days it takes for growth to be observed, the teacher makes a green rectangle on today's date on the calendar. "This will help us to remember when we planted our bulb," she explains.

The next day the teacher brings the potted bulb to the meeting area for more analysis. "What do you notice today?" she begins.

ROSIE: Nothing has happened.
RAY: The book said it would take a long time.
STEVE: I didn't think anything would happen.
TEACHER: HOW TALL IS OUR PLANT?

As the teacher anticipated, the children are confused by the question. Their expressions suggest that they believe that such an inquiry is not yet relevant. But the teacher posed the question to set the stage for later work.

TEACHER: HOW MANY DAYS HAS THE PLANT BEEN GROWING?

Again, the children are silent. The teacher wonders if their silence is related to the idea that they can't see plant growth yet. She offers a different question.

TEACHER: HOW MANY DAYS HAS IT BEEN SINCE WE PLANTED OUR BULB?
PATSY: One.
RAY: No, two—today and yesterday.

A class debate ensues about how to correctly answer this question. Is it one or two days? The teacher is not surprised by these conflicting ideas. She has come to realize that this seemingly straightforward question isn't as simple as it appears. How to deal with "end points" is an important mathematical consideration. Deciding whether to count the first day or to wait until twenty-four hours have passed presents a challenge. After discussion, the children decide that the plant has been planted for one day. "How can we keep track of the number of days?" asks the teacher.

Chuck suggests, "We could use cubes like we do for the days of school. We just have to keep them different." The other children agree with Chuck's idea and a special place is designated to keep the train of cubes that will be formed for this purpose. The teacher asks several students to select these cubes. The children talk among themselves as they complete the task.

JANE: How many should we get?
PATSY: I think we'll need more than ten, maybe a hundred.
RALPH: The book said it would take a long time to grow.
KYLE: I don't think I can count to one hundred.
JANE: We can do as much as we can.

The children present their teacher with a cup filled to the top with Unifix cubes. They decided not to count them; the amount in the cup seems sufficient for the task. Most kindergarten children are not ready to count large quantities accurately, but recognize the importance of magnitude. Whether they need more or less cubes will be determined as the days unfold and the plant grows.

For the next several days, the class focuses on adding one more cube to the train each day. This process keeps the experiment alive for the time during which the plant shows no visible growth. Throughout the day, they occasionally wander to the far side of the room to check the bulb on the windowsill. Sometimes they go alone, sometimes in pairs, or groups of three. An often-heard remark is, "Do you think this will ever grow?"

Three and a half weeks have passed when the teacher brings the plant back to the meeting area for careful examination and discussion. Though subtle, growth is now evident. A small green tip has emerged from the bulb.

TEACHER: WHAT DO YOU NOTICE?
MAKEITHA: You can see some green. Is that the plant?

ROSIE: That looks just like the book. (Rosie finds the copy of *A Flower Grows* and opens to a page that indeed looks similar to the class plant at this stage.)

RAY: It's small, but it's going.

SIDDARTH: It *is* growing.

The children demonstrate their astonishment at this development. Though they had been anticipating the change, they are still surprised by the reality of it, perhaps due to the long wait.

The teacher wants to bring up the idea of measurement again. She inquires, "How tall is our plant?" Silence fills the room. She decides to stimulate the children's thinking. She has brought a bucket of cubes with her and asks, "What if we used our cubes to help us?"

Harold responds, "I think we need ten." The teacher motions for Harold to test his prediction. He snaps ten cubes together and stands them next to the flowerpot.

Siddarth looks puzzled. Finally he says, "That's too much. I think you just need the green part." The teacher encourages Siddarth to show the class what he is thinking.

Siddarth snaps two cubes together and stands them at the base of where you can see the green sprout emerge from the bulb. "That's too big," he concludes. He takes one cube and tries again, locating his measuring device in the same location.

Ray remains unconvinced. "I think you need more," he announces. The teacher asks him why he thinks this. "You need to do the whole thing," he replies, and moves to demonstrate his idea. He snaps together three cubes and stands them next to where the bulb emerges from the soil. A brief discussion follows.

TEACHER: I THINK THIS IS VERY INTERESTING. WE HAVE SEEN THREE DIFFERENT WAYS TO MEASURE OUR PLANT. DOES IT MATTER HOW WE DO IT?

SIDDARTH: Yes, you can only measure the plant, the green part.

CORRINE: The bulb is part of the plant. I agree with Ray.

HAROLD: I guess I did too much. The pot is big.

The children begin to fidget and the teacher decides not to pursue the matter further. Before the end of the day, each child completes another observation for his or her log.

Teacher Reflection

I asked the children about the height of the plant in the very beginning of our experiment. At first, they had no idea why I was asking this question. But I thought it was important to talk about this right away, and I was curious if anyone would suggest measuring the pot or the exposed bulb at that point.

I was excited about today's conversation. The children are now focusing on the importance of establishing a starting point. At this time, it doesn't matter whether or not they each choose the same one, but rather, that they each make a conscious decision about what should be included in the height.

Later, I want the children to compare their measures taken at different points in time. To do so, the children must recognize the need to always measure from the same end point. If I would just tell them where to measure from on the plant, it would be easy. Most children would follow the directions. But they wouldn't really know why this aspect of measurement is so important. I'd rather wait to see what ideas the children formulate themselves. I don't want to steal this learning opportunity from them. By leaving it more open, however, I know that it could get "messy." Some children, for example, might find a length that is shorter the second time they measure.

I enjoyed looking at their log entries. Each child made a picture of the plant showing a tip of green. I was pleased to see how realistically they tried to make their drawings. I know how tempting it is to use a favorite color rather than to look carefully and decide to be as accurate as possible. I know the children will become even more interested in our project now that change has taken place that they can see.

Once the tiny green shoot begins to show, the plant seems to change almost daily. The children continue to record their observations and to take this task seriously. Within their drawings, they strive to replicate the way the plant looks as best they can. They look at shape and placement of new growth and try to capture every detail.

On this day, the children are asked to measure the height of the plant and to represent their work in an observation report. They work individually or in pairs over the course of the day. Katrina begins by snapping eight cubes together. Like many children, she seems to have an expectation as to how many cubes will be needed. She holds the stack next to the plant. "No, too short," she says aloud, and adds one more cube to her stack. She counts the cubes, removing one from her stack each time she verbalizes a number name. She then draws a picture (see Figure 7–1) of the nine cubes in their unconnected form.

Tristen begins by making a tall stack of cubes. He doesn't count them; he just connects them until, apparently, he thinks he has enough. He places the stack next to the plant on top of the soil. "Oops," he exclaims and removes approximately a third of the stack. He counts the remaining cubes and records the numeral 10. It is not uncommon for children to record only a

---

Observation Sheet

We planted an amaryllis bulb on January 2.
This is what it looks like today.

FIGURE 7–1 *Katrina's work*

numerical answer. His teacher, however, wants her students to begin to understand the idea that a measurement must give a number as well as indicate the unit of measurement that was used. She wants to encourage Tristen to go further with his response. "How will people looking at your paper know what that number means?" she asks. Tristen puts the stack of cubes on his paper and traces it. He looks at his results for awhile as if trying to decide what to do next. He then draws ten horizontal lines (unwittingly creating eleven rectangles) to represent ten cubes (see Figure 7–2).

In their responses, several of the other children also trace their stacks. For many, this technique requires that they then

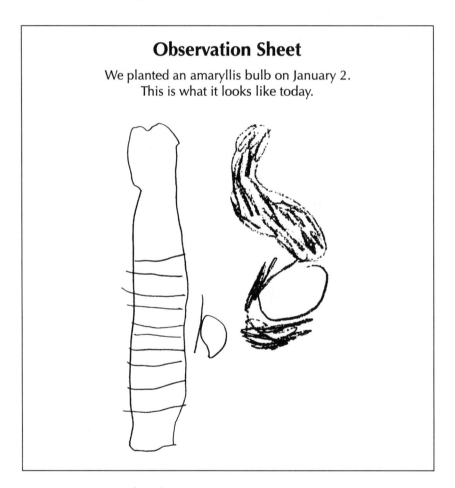

FIGURE 7–2   *Tristen's work*

grapple with how to subdivide the whole. They know how many units they have and their outlines tell them how much space their cubes take on their papers, but they're unsure of how to show the individual units. There is much use of erasers when this happens. Some children become frustrated and doubtful of how to reconcile their ideas. Phil looks at his outline, picks up his pencil, and then puts it down. He looks again and picks up his pencil, and then shakes his head. He leaves the outline as is and then records the number of cubes in his stack. (See Figure 7–3.)

Angelina places one cube on top of the bulb. "You only want to do the green part," she explains to her partner, Rocky. Rocky then hands her the cubes, one at a time, and she adds them onto her original cube. They work this way until they agree that their stack is as long as the shoot. They count the number of

FIGURE 7–3   *Phil's work*

cubes in the stack together. Rocky moves his finger down the stack as Angela says a number. They then make their recordings separately. Angela's recording (Figure 7–4) shows that she has written a number in each cube.

Alan begins his recording at the bottom right of his observation sheet, by drawing three cubes connected by two lines. Glancing around him, he sees that his neighbor is drawing his cubes next to one another. Alan then mimics this technique (see Figure 7–5), drawing four cubes to the left of his first three. He writes a number in each cube and, realizing he's two short, adds them in a top row, numbering these as well.

FIGURE 7–4   *Angelina's work*

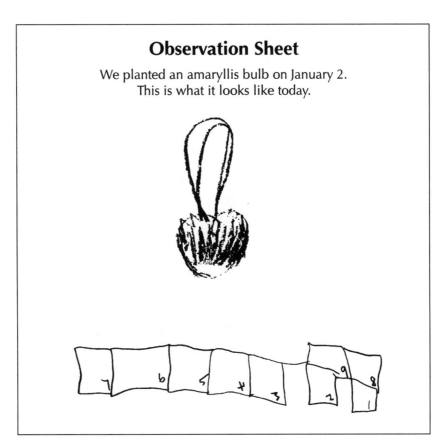

Observation Sheet

We planted an amaryllis bulb on January 2.
This is what it looks like today.

FIGURE 7–5   *Alan's work*

The recording sheets don't allow the children to make a picture of the plant that is actually nine or ten cubes high (unless they draw over the words at the top of the page). Most children represent the cubes as close to their actual size and render the plant as smaller than it in fact is. They don't seem bothered by the fact that their pictures of the stacks are not the same heights as their depicted plants. Lee, however, takes particular care to show the cubes lined up along the shoot (see Figure 7–6). In order to do so, he has drawn cubes of a smaller size.

Corrine's thinking is somewhat unique. In fact, in the years that the teacher has conducted this activity, she has not seen another child record her work in a similar manner. Once she forms her stack of cubes, Corrine puts the stack on her paper and draws a line the length of its edge (see Figure 7–7). "It's like a

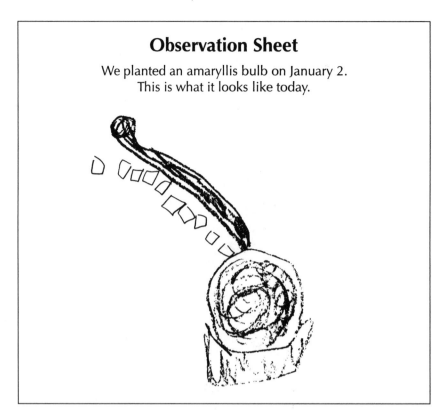

FIGURE 7–6   *Lee's work*

ruler," she proclaims, suggesting that she has a somewhat more abstract view of measurement than her peers do.

No one is too fussy about exactly where on the plant they place their stacks of cubes, but the children understand what they are doing and take their work seriously. Since the first discussion, no one places the cubes alongside the bottom of the flowerpot. What's most important is that they are paying attention to a starting point. This is a significant step in their ability to make more accurate measurements. Some children use nine cubes and others ten. One child arrives at an answer of eight cubes. This differentiation does not concern the children when they compare their results. Some of this variation is due to whether children add a cube to show lengths smaller than the cube unit or disregard growth that cannot be represented by a whole cube. No one suggests using a fraction of a cube.

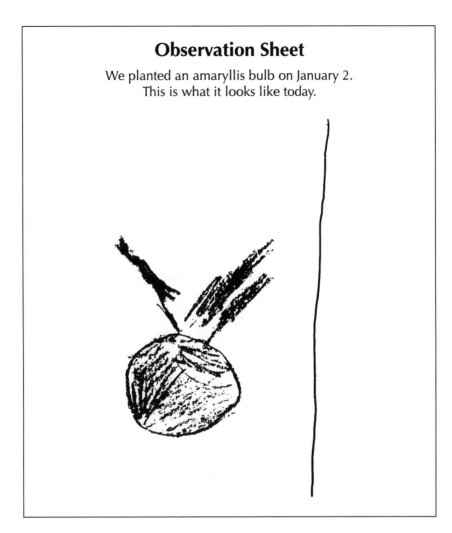

Observation Sheet

We planted an amaryllis bulb on January 2.
This is what it looks like today.

FIGURE 7–7   *Corrine's work*

The work with the amaryllis plant takes place over eight weeks. The children measure the growth, look for changes, and continue to add cubes daily to note the number of days that have passed since the bulb was planted. They add details to their drawings to illustrate buds that develop, and later, blossoms that appear. As the children sharpen their observational skills, they learn that the mathematical ideas of counting, comparison, and one-to-one matching support their scientific endeavors. They continue to record their observations until the blossoms have wilted. They look carefully at the place on the shoot that swells and are surprised to find seeds inside.

The unit is a success on many levels. These young children have had an opportunity to see the cycle of nature at work in their classroom. They have begun to realize the importance of charting growth over time. They have progressed from their instinctual desires to snap together long trains of cubes to using these objects as nonstandard measurement units.

Kindergarten offers many opportunities for informal measurement as well. Having sand or water tables in the room allows for children to compare volume and weight. Their conversations as they pour and sift help them to integrate phrases such as *holds more, holds less, heavier,* and *lighter* into their everyday language. Balance scales, available during exploration time, support simple investigations such as, *Can you find something to balance an apple? Can you find three things that together are lighter than an apple?* The dramatic play area also stimulates the growth of measurement concepts and vocabulary as the children pretend to cook on the stove, shop in the store, or compare the length of dress-up shoes. These active explorations are critical to students' development of comparative language and emerging ideas of measurement.

How can this active learning about measurement continue in the first grade, when so much is expected of six- and seven-year-olds, when classrooms are more structured, and when the focus tends to be primarily on literacy learning?

A Bakery

One first-grade teacher vowed that her classroom would always have some sort of dramatic play area. She wanted her students to have opportunities for play and imagination while applying their emerging skills to authentic learning situations (things they might see or do in the real world). For several years, a classroom "bakery" has served this purpose. The bakery provides her students with many opportunities to apply their newly acquired literacy skills and strategies. They read lists of ingredients, follow simple directions, decipher ways in which measurements are recorded, and make signs announcing what is being sold. Furthermore, the children make considerable gains in their abilities to communicate with each other and to work cooperatively.

The cooking projects also promote mathematical skills. The children measure using measuring spoons and cups, become familiar with the symbol for one-half, and work with money.

This year, the bakery began in early December. The children had been reading several books by Eric Carle to coincide with an author study about Carle's life and works. When they became interested in the book *Walter the Baker*, Latisha said, "I wish we could have a bakery." The teacher then asked the students if they would like to open a bakery in their class. She was pleased since, as with the first year she had a bakery in her classroom, the idea came from the children rather than herself. The other students responded with immediate enthusiasm and quickly found ways to relate personally to this new idea.

HAL: I like to help my mom bake cookies.

MARTINA: My dad is a chef, maybe he can help us.

LISA: My big sister works at a pizza place. She can show us how to throw the pizza in the air.

SIMON: I like to go to Dunkin Donuts with my brother. I love doughnuts.

In the days that follow, several steps are taken to get ready for the bakery. A location in the room is identified as well as furniture for the counter and storage area. A letter is sent home explaining the project and asking for parents to volunteer ingredients and time. The children debate the name of the bakery and this year decide to call it Delicious Dishes. They discuss baked goods that they want to make and sell. They look through cookbooks and set up a play cash register equipped with play money. Surveys are taken to ask classmates about their favorite kinds of baked goods. Finally, signs are made to announce the grand opening.

Each day the bakery is opened a new staff is identified. Jobs include being the store manager, bakers, sales clerks, and assistants. The children bake once or twice each week, for about two months, so that everyone gets a chance to be involved. As everyone wants to help, a chart of bakery workers is created. In the morning, during their literacy block, one group opens the bakery and works on making the wares for the day. Usually these items come from donations of mixes and other perishable items. In the afternoon during math workshop, the bakery opens again so that the wares can be sold. The children are earnest about their jobs and of course everyone loves to eat the baked goods that are made.

One day in mid-January, Angelo, Latisha, Mary, and Francisco are preparing to bake. They decide that they will bake a cake; a chocolate cake mix is chosen. A parent is present to facilitate the experience.

Latisha announces, "We need a big bowl to put the things in." Francisco volunteers to get the bowl.

Angelo focuses on the cake mix, looking at the directions on the back of the box. "Mary," he asks, "What does this say?"

Mary leads the group in deciphering that eggs and oil are needed. Latisha has found a large bowl for mixing the batter and Angelo has pulled out both a 9-by-13-inch baking dish and a cupcake pan.

ANGELO: Which do we use?

MARY: Are we making a cake or cupcakes?

LATISHA: Let's make a cake.

FRANCISCO: No, let's make cupcakes, then everyone gets the same.

PARENT: What do you mean?

FRANCISCO: If you make a cake you have to cut the pieces. It is hard. When you make cupcakes, you just make twenty-six.

PARENT: Why twenty-six?

MARY: We need one for everyone in the class. We have twenty-six kids.

LATISHA: We need more so that you can have one (referring to the parent helper) and our teacher, too. We need twenty-eight.

PARENT: Can you cut the cake into twenty-eight pieces?

ANGELO: I guess you can, but it is hard. Everyone complains if their piece is small. Let's make cupcakes.

FRANCISCO: Cupcakes is good. It's like they're already measured. *[The children begin to assemble the ingredients listed in the recipe.]*

MARY: How much oil do we need?

FRANCISCO: What does the box say?

LATISHA: It says two spoons.

ANGELO: How big are the spoons?

LATISHA: You know, the big ones.

PARENT: When I bake at home I try to be exact and follow the recipe. It says you need two tablespoons of oil. Does anyone know how much that is?

The children begin to look around at the various measuring cups and spoons that are kept in the storage area. Francisco and Mary compare a tablespoon and a teaspoon. Mary announces that hers is bigger.

The children look carefully at the markings on the spoons and choose the correct one. Angelo pours in one tablespoon of oil. Latisha pours the other.

The children have learned to refer to the directions on the box as their recipe. They follow each step carefully. Soon the mix is ready to be poured into the cupcake tins to prepare for baking. The children are industrious and full of chatter.

MARY: Do we have to turn on the oven?

PARENT: Yes, we need to preheat the oven. Your teacher said we would use the oven in the teacher's room. Would you like to go with me to do that?

MARY: Let me look at the box so we know how much.

FRANCISCO: How much what?

MARY: How much to turn the oven on.

FRANCISCO: You mean how high.

MARY: We need to turn on the oven so we can bake the cupcakes.

FRANCISCO: The number on the box tells you how high to make it.

PARENT: Yes, Francisco, maybe you would like to go with us. Latisha and Angelo, would you begin to clean up?

Even in these brief exchanges, it is clear that the bakery provides many opportunities for these first graders to explore a variety of measurement concepts. They considered relative size and the need for precision. They pondered the fairness of measures in deciding to bake cupcakes rather than a cake. They identified the correct tool for measuring a tablespoon and considered vocabulary as it relates to temperature. Throughout the unit, the children are constantly integrating new skills even though they see the bakery as play.

Later in the day, a new team of children rotates into the bakery and prepares to open it to sell the cupcakes. They establish their roles: Li is the stock clerk, Rosie is the store manager, Lance is the cashier, and Katlin is the assistant. Li places the cupcakes on paper napkins so that classmates can purchase them. Lance and Katlin set up the cash register and ledger along with cups of coins for student use. They know that the team needs to decide on the price for the cupcakes before they can open the bakery.

ROSIE: How much will the cupcakes be?

LANCE: On Monday the cookies were seven cents each. I think a cupcake is bigger than a cookie.

KATLIN: Me, too. How about fourteen cents? A cupcake is like having two cookies and seven plus seven is fourteen.

LI: That's a lot of pennies.

TEACHER: WHAT DO YOU MEAN?

LI: Well, fourteen is a lot of pennies that everyone needs.

KATLIN: But they can give us different than fourteen pennies. They can give us a dime and four pennies. That's fourteen.

LANCE: Or a dime and a nickel is fifteen cents. Let's make it fifteen.

LI: Maybe we should just make it fifteen cents. It will be easier.

TEACHER: WHAT DO YOU MEAN EASIER?

LI: We won't need many pennies.

TEACHER: IS THAT TRUE?

ROSIE: Yes.

KATLIN: No. They could still give us fifteen pennies.

LI : Or a quarter.

ROSIE: Let's make it fifteen.

Soon Rosie announces to the class that the bakery is open for business. While the afternoon team has been preparing to open, their classmates have been attending to other math workshop choices. Though many have the impulse to run right over when the announcement is made, they have learned to wait for the store manager to ask a few children at a time if they would like to purchase something from the bakery. It is certainly appropriate if they say no thank you and of course precautions are made to consider dietary restrictions of classmates. There are always alternative items available, such as bread and trail mix for children with allergies or whose parents have asked that intake of sweets be limited.

Lance and Katlin are ready to take orders. They place dishes of coins on the table so that their classmates can "pay" for their goods. Katlin keeps a tally of the number of items sold. Li replenishes supplies when needed and continues to make sure that cupcakes are served with a napkin.

Steve comes to the counter and says, "I would like a cupcake please. I have fifteen cents." He then hands Lance the fifteen pennies he just counted out from the community dishes of coins.

Lance double-checks the count and says, "thank you," while Katlin places one tally mark on the ledger. She has previously dated the page, printed the word *cupcake*, and written "15¢," to signify the amount being charged today.

Zoe is next and gives Lance two dimes. She explains, "I would like one with chocolate frosting, please. I have fifteen cents."

"I think this is twenty cents, two dimes, right?" replies Lance.

"Oops," responds Zoe, " I thought I gave you a dime and a nickel. Two dimes is twenty cents."

Lance turns to Katlin, "How much do we need?"

Katlin replies, "Twenty is more than fifteen. Zoe, give back one of the dimes and get a nickel."

Zoe returns the dime, takes a nickel, and proudly returns to the bakery announcing, "I have a dime and a nickel, that's fifteen cents."

This type of cooperative exchange continues until all customers have been serviced. Finally, the students who have been running the bakery get a chance to purchase their cupcakes. The bakers are thanked, ideas are shared about future bakery items, and a tally of the daily sales is made. Before the bakery closes for the day, the afternoon team makes sure that everything is cleaned up and the CLOSED sign is hung.

Teacher Reflection

The original idea for the bakery came from the students a few years ago. I recognized that I could figure out a purposeful way to include money in the work. It is one thing for children to see icons of coins on a worksheet and to circle the correct value, it is quite another to learn to make collections of real coins to match a given cost.

From the start of school I use coins as one way to represent the number of days in school when we record that data daily. We begin by adding a penny for each day. Soon we learn to exchange five pennies for a nickel, and five pennies and a nickel for two nickels or a dime. This daily exposure helps set the stage for our use of money in the bakery.

During the first few sales of the year, I have only pennies available. Next we add dimes and nickels, and finally quarters. Each team of children working in the bakery sets the price of the items. I marvel at how quickly they select prices based on previous experience—as, for example, since the cookie was seven cents, the cupcake is valued at fifteen cents, since it is bigger. It is exciting to see their ideas as consumers emerge as well. Inevitably, to these first-grade students, bigger means it has to cost more.

In order for the children to actually purchase the wares, I have set up dishes of coins by denomination. As the children enter the bakery, they need to select the coins they think will allow them to make their purchases. In this way, every child gets a little practice each day.

Mostly, I just let the bakery run its course. The authentic nature of having students "pay" for their baked goods is a worthy idea in first-grade classrooms. It has not been my expectation that first graders be able to make change, but rather, that they learn to identify coins in context and be able to count out the correct amount in order to purchase their treats. However, there are times that I have manipulated the math in order to challenge my most advanced students or to broaden learning for all students. I might give one child a particular set of coins that will require change to be made. I might also take away dimes to simulate what happens when you run short of one type of coin.

I am always so pleased to see the bakery in action. The children seem to thrive on these types of real-world experiences. Over the years, the bakery has enabled many mathematical and literacy experiences to be brought into focus. The children never cease to amaze me.

A Sense of Units

In their daily conversations, you can hear second-grade students begin to use measurement in their descriptions. In one second-grade class, students are talking about the height of snow piles they passed on their way to school. This conversation takes place at snack time on the day after a snowstorm that caused school to be canceled.

EMILIO: We have a lot of snow on my street.
RAMONA: When I was walking to school, it was over my leg.
[As Ramona speaks she places her hand next to her hip. Her palm faces the floor as she shows her classmates the height of the snow bank.]
LISA: That's a lot. How high is that?
RAMONA: I want to measure.
KIM SU: Let's get a ruler.
EMILIO: How about a yardstick? It is bigger. It will be easier to tell.

The children in this classroom feel comfortable to pursue their mathematical conversation and subsequent experiment during snack time. They independently find a yardstick and measure the height of Ramona's hand when she again places it near her body to show the height of the snow bank.

KIM SU: It says thirty-one inches.

RAMONA: Wow, that is a lot. I am fifty-two inches tall. We always measure on my birthday.

LISA: How many feet?

KIM SU: Thirty-one inches, hmm, maybe three feet. Twelve and twelve is twenty-four, so it's more than that. Maybe three feet.

RAMONA: No, three feet is thirty-six inches—twelve plus twelve plus twelve. So it's not three feet.

EMILIO: Since one foot of snow is twelve inches, two feet is twenty-four inches. You need twenty-five, twenty-six, twenty-seven, twenty-eight, twenty-nine, thirty, thirty-one [while counting on his fingers]—that's seven more inches. So it's two feet, seven inches.

Knowing that there are twelve inches in a foot provides a way for these children to think about the number of inches in two or three feet. They also are able to decide what to do with remaining inches that don't make an entire foot. At this point, they seem satisfied with Emilio's answer and their snack time conversation turns to making snowmen and going sledding.

It is certainly not the case that all second graders can, or would, participate in such a conversation. But second grade can be a time when children begin to explore measurement in a more formal way. It is a time when children's sense of the various units of measure can begin to deepen.

Classroom measurement activities should support this growth. They should provide students with opportunities to utilize their number awareness, to think about the relative magnitude of numbers and units, to develop benchmarks that can help them to estimate measures, and to measure real objects. Conversations help children to wrestle with these ideas and to solidify their thinking. To further stimulate conversations about measurement, their teacher introduced this second-grade class to the problem shown in Figure 7–8.

Write the measurements that make the most sense.

6 miles	50 inches	2 yards
18 inches	10 feet	7 inches

Jake likes to play basketball. His hoop is _____ high.
He also likes to draw at the kitchen table. The table is
_____ long. He uses colored pencils that are
_____ long.

Jake has a new baby sister. She is _____ long. Jake's
dad is _____ tall. He likes to run. He just won a road
race that was _____ long.

FIGURE 7–8   *Measurement problem about Jake*

The students first read the problem together as a class. When the teacher is confident that the children understand the problem, she gives each one a copy. The children then begin to work individually, in pairs, or in small groups. The room quickly fills with lively conversations about Jake, the character featured in the problem. Questions, strategies, and conjectures begin to emerge.

TYRONE: Can you use more than one answer?

ALBA: Yeah, the table and the hoop could be the same if the hoop was one of those little ones.

TYRONE: No, I know a basketball hoop is ten feet tall. There is one at the park. My uncle told me how tall it was.

IRENA: Where do we start?

CONRAD: I have a baby brother. He was twenty-one inches long when he was born. I think eighteen inches is a good guess for that one.

ALISON: I did the basketball hoop as the first one because I knew it. My brother plays basketball and he knows a lot about it. He told me.

Once the students have an opportunity to think about the problem, sort out possible solutions, and make their decisions, a whole-class meeting is held so that ideas can be shared and solutions confirmed.

TEACHER: I'M CURIOUS. HOW DID YOU GO ABOUT SOLVING THIS PROBLEM?

RAMONA: I sort of went around. Then I didn't like what I had because everything didn't exactly fit in. So then I kept going around and making changes.

TEACHER: DOES EVERYONE KNOW WHAT RAMONA MEANS BY "WENT AROUND?"

STEVE: Yeah, I did that too. I just kept reading the problem and trying different numbers. I kept going around and around with my ideas.

TEACHER: WAS IT JUST THE NUMBERS THAT YOU HAD TO TRY?

WILL: No, you had to know about the words. Like feet and inches. I had to keep thinking about how big.

RAOUL: Me too. I thought about which thing was the biggest.

TEACHER: WHAT DID YOU DECIDE?

JUSTINA: The road race has to be the biggest. It's six miles.

TEACHER: IS EVERYBODY SURE THAT THE ROAD RACE IS SIX MILES?

[Students nod, gesture, and voice agreement.]

BEN: I think it has to be six miles because it couldn't be all the others.

JAYLEEN: Because you can't be six miles long. It has to be a road. Miles is always a clue. You can't be six miles tall or six miles wide. It's got to be a road. I know. I go to my grandmother's and every time I always think miles.

SEAN: That's process of elimination. My mom told me that. It couldn't be the rest. It has to be miles.

JANEEN: All those other ones mean something straight, but a mile feels like it could be curvy.

EMILIO: Ten feet is from here to the other side of the classroom, so that couldn't be long enough for a race.

The conversation takes a turn away from the problem as classmates begin to debate with Emilio about whether the length of the classroom is ten feet. There is much speculation and disagreement.

Andrew suggests, "The classroom is a lot bigger than ten feet. I think we should measure. One step is like a foot. Remember we read that book about the king's bed? I'll show you it's more than ten."

When new ideas arise in the classroom, teachers need to make quick decisions about whether to move the conversation in that direction or to stay with the initial problem. On this day the teacher decides to take Andrew's suggestion, hoping that by pacing off the room quickly, Emilio and others would see that indeed it was longer than ten feet. She encourages Andrew to show what he is thinking. After the demonstration Emilio agrees with Andrew.

TEACHER: WE'VE BEEN TALKING A LOT ABOUT THE TEN FEET. LET'S LOOK BACK AT THE PROBLEM ABOUT JAKE. WHICH ONE OF THE ANSWERS IS TEN FEET?

ALISON: I know that ten feet is the basketball hoop.

BOBBY: I looked up there [at the wall measurement] and knew four more feet, because it goes up to six feet. So six and four is ten feet and that seems as tall as a basketball hoop. They are really tall.

TEACHER: DOES EVERYONE AGREE ABOUT THE RACE AND THE BASKETBALL HOOP?

[Students signal that they do.]

TEACHER: WHAT ELSE ARE YOU CONVINCED OF OR SURE ABOUT?

RAMONA: I did the pencil next. That one is the smallest. It's seven inches.

BEN: A baby could be seven inches, too. *[A discussion about how big babies are when they are born ensues.]*

JAYLEEN: The baby is seven inches. Newborn babies are small. A new baby can't be eighteen inches.

RAMONA: I'm not sure, but it doesn't mean it's just out of the hospital. It could be five months old.

WILL: My baby sister was twenty inches long I think. I think seven is too small.

ELLIS: It's eighteen inches for the baby.

JAYLEEN: If you say so.

As the children come to agreement about each measure, their teacher records the answers on an enlarged copy of the problem. At this point they have filled in *10 feet* for the basketball hoop, *7 inches* for the pencil, *18 inches* for the baby, and *6 miles* for the road race.

TEACHER: WE HAVE TWO BLANKS LEFT.

RAMONA: How can a dad be two somethings tall?

GINNY: This one is hard.

WILL: You got to look at the yards.

EMILIO: I know how to figure out a yard—three plus three equals six. So that's six feet.

SEAN: How big is that?

KIM SU: I figured it out. I added twelve, six times, and I got seventy-two.

RAMONA: My dad is six feet.

STEVE: It couldn't be fifty inches. I'm more than fifty inches.

TEACHER: DOES THAT MAKE SENSE? DO YOUR DADS SEEM ABOUT TWO YARDS OR SIX FEET TALL? *[Heads nod in agreement.]*

STEVE: Two yards sounds funny for the dad but when you make it feet it is OK.

STEVE: Then the table is fifty inches.

TEACHER: LET'S READ IT WITH ALL THE NUMBERS INCLUDED. *[The children read the completed problem together.]*

These second graders are gaining a sense of the various units we use to measure length and their relative sizes. Comments such as, "All those other ones mean something straight, but a mile feels like it could be curvy," provide us insight into how some children differentiate shorter and longer lengths. "Two yards sounds funny for the dad but when you make it feet it is OK," suggests that even children at this young age recognize that we usually indicate adults' height in feet. Making sense of this problem helps children gain confidence in their understanding of measurement ideas and illustrates the importance of relating new ideas to previous knowledge.

Teacher Reflection

I was delighted to hear children rely on their previous knowledge as they worked to make sense of this problem. They referred to Rolf Myler's story, *How Big Is a Foot?*, their own height and the height of relatives, and what some knew as factual, such as the height of a basketball hoop. I was also glad to hear Bobby refer to the height chart on our door and I saw several children take out rulers in order to decide on the length of the pencil. I want measurement tools to be accessible to my students and for them to feel comfortable using them at all times. If they can think through the problem by estimating, that is fine, too.

When the children were working on their own, I heard comments such as, "I'm writing light in pencil in case I need to change it around." They were engaged in this task, worked with each other, and incorporated some of the simple measuring techniques we have discussed. I saw several children use their fingers to form an inch and then compare that seven times to the pencil they were using. It was fun to watch this in action.

I want my students to have many opportunities to both measure and to estimate measurements. I want them to gain their own set of benchmarks so they have something to refer to when someone asks, "How tall is that?" It's important that I help them to build on their intuitive ideas. They will use measurement for the rest of their lives.

8

Seeing Patterns and Sharing Algebraic Ideas

I t is not uncommon for an adult to sigh mournfully upon hearing the word *algebra*. For many, the mere mention of algebra brings to mind unpleasant memories of mindless manipulation of symbols and of trying to solve problems that seemed irrelevant and frustrating. Now we are being asked to explore algebraic thinking throughout the grades. Why do we need to do so? How is it possible to introduce algebraic concepts in ways that make sense for young children who are just learning about numbers? How does talking with children about their ideas and having them represent their thoughts with manipulatives or on paper help them to develop their algebraic thinking?

Algebra is sometimes referred to as a gatekeeper, emphasizing the fact that many students are kept out of further study of mathematics or closed off from later employment opportunities due to lack of algebraic skills. This "gate" needs to be open to males and females of all racial and ethnic groups. Current research supports the idea that early exposure to algebraic thinking will help students gain the skills, concepts, and experiences they need to keep the gate open. We also know that, as in all areas of mathematics, the communication and representation of ideas can deepen the internalization of those ideas. This internal understanding can then in turn provide the foundation for future exploration and success.

Algebraic thinking has been embedded in the early-childhood curriculum for many years. It can be a challenge for primary teachers, however, to recognize how and when algebraic thinking comes into play. To solve story problems, children model mathematical relationships with physical materials, pictures, and symbols. This is the essence of early algebraic thinking. When children explore addition expressions such as 3 + 5 and 5 + 3, and determine that the order doesn't change the sum, they are using their observations to make an important generalization about addition. Children often invent their own vocabulary to explore the commutative property ("when you add, opposites always give the same answer"). Later, this property can be represented by the simple algebraic statement, $x + y = y + x$.

Patterns are a common topic in early-childhood classrooms. When children explore patterns, they have opportunities to investigate and extend relationships, make conjectures, and form generalizations. As teachers, if we can be clear on how pattern activities involve algebraic thinking, we can nurture children's emerging ideas.

Repeating Patterns

Repeating patterns involve the cyclical repetition of an identifiable unit or core. For example, if you clap your hands, snap your fingers, clap your hands, and snap your fingers, you are repeating the unit "clap, snap" for two cycles. Young children copy, extend, create, translate, describe, represent, and generalize repeating patterns without realizing that these activities are fundamental components of algebraic thinking. Consider this example from a kindergarten classroom.

This class begins to explore patterns early in the fall. Initially, the patterns emerge from the children's free play with teddy bear counters, cubes, and tiles. Children naturally alternate colors when they work with these materials. The patterns aren't necessarily followed consistently, but the arrangements tend to contain sections of, for example, alternating blues and yellows, allowing the teacher to ask, "What comes next? How do you know?" Soon the children focus on extending these color patterns. Linked cubes may be joined across the room in a systematic arrangement of two or three colors.

Over the course of the year, children generate patterns with numerous types of manipulative materials. They listen to clapping rhythms and try to repeat them. They attempt to follow along with gesture games that instruct them to do such things as "touch your shoulders, touch your knees, touch your shoulders, touch you knees." They create their own patterns and continue their classmates' patterns.

One day, the children are sitting on a rug in a circle. Their teacher asks if they can form a girl, boy pattern—an arrangement they recognize as an alternating pattern. The request is familiar to this class of five- and six-year-olds, who often are asked to create or continue a pattern when they first form a circle or are transitioning from one activity to another. The children respond to the task immediately.

FRED: Erica, sit next to me.
MEI: No, I already have a boy [motioning to Nicky, who is sitting to her left].
TORI: But we can't go together. We're the same. [Tori is sitting to Erica's right.]
ERICA: OK. I forgot about both sides.
NANCY: I need a boy here.
MARC: I can move between Carlita and Mei.

This activity continues as the children help each other reposition themselves to satisfy the conditions of the pattern.

COLIN: Wait, it won't work. We have more boys than girls.
TEACHER: WHAT DO YOU MEAN?
VIV: Yeah, Dawn is absent and so we have too many boys. I don't think it will work either.

Due to their familiarity with AB patterns, the children are able to make some interesting generalizations. Tori recognizes that two of the same element (two boys or two girls) can't be together in an AB pattern. Colin and Viv suggest that such a pattern requires the same number of each element (boys and girls). This conversation demonstrates that young children are able to go beyond making observations about specific configurations (such as, "This pattern is a red, blue pattern") and can think in the abstract about conditions that hold for all AB patterns.

A significant task for kindergarten children is to recognize that a sit, stand pattern has the same AB structure as a red, yellow pattern, but is not the same as a red, yellow, green (ABC) pattern. Recognizing families of patterns is an important aspect of algebraic thinking. It involves making a generalization after examining several specific cases. Referring to these families as, for example, AB or AAB patterns involves the symbolic notation of this mathematical idea. Challenging students to translate a red, green, green (ABB) pattern made with linked cubes to a pattern made with different colors or materials helps children to identify the essence of the pattern. As is demonstrated in the following situation, talk that emerges naturally as children compare their patterns provides opportunities for children to wrestle with ideas and to further develop generalizations.

Shaina and Kelsey are working side by side, though they are each engrossed in their individual work. Shaina has placed fifteen color tiles in an ABC pattern. Her "color train," as she refers to it, is made up of five repetitions of green, blue, and red. Kelsey has also made a color train including the colors green and blue. He has made an ABB pattern (green, blue, blue). At one point Kelsey looks at Shaina's work and makes the following claim.

KELSEY: Hey, we made the same pattern.
SHAINA: We did. Oh, no we didn't. They are the same, but mine has red. See? *[Shaina points to a red tile in her pattern.]*
KELSEY: But it goes green, blue *[pointing to the first two tiles in Shaina's work]* and green, blue *[pointing to the first two tiles in his own work]*.
SHAINA: But mine is green, blue, *red*; green, blue, *red*; green, blue, *red*; green, blue, *red*; green, blue, *red*. Yours is green, blue, *blue*; green, blue, *blue*; green, blue, *blue*; green, blue, *blue*; green, blue, *blue*.
KELSEY: Well, they both have green, blue! But I guess you have red, too.

It is clear that Kelsey recognizes that the first two elements in the two patterns are the same. He might also see that both patterns have three elements. Shaina is trying to convince him that the overall patterns are different. Her determined verbalization suggests that she believes she can convince Kelsey of what she knows through her command of ideas and language. Kelsey appears more interested in how their patterns are the same than different, but his ideas did shift somewhat. Giving children ample opportunities to share their emerging ideas, debate possible conjectures, and learn from one another has immense value.

In first and second grades, children can explore more complex ideas about repeating patterns; for example, they can investigate the relationship between an element of a pattern, such as the color of a chip, and the element's position within that pattern. Consider the following activity in a first-grade classroom. The teacher wants her students to make predictions about what happens when a repeated pattern is extended. She begins this math session by having the children follow her in a clap, snap pattern.

TEACHER: WHAT ARE WE DOING?

KIMI: It's a pattern: clap, snap, clap, snap.

BENITA: It's a pattern because you're going one, two, one, two, one, two.

TEACHER: HOW DO YOU KNOW?

BENITA: It's not the same as clap, clap, or one, one. It's clap, snap, clap, snap. It repeats.

KEIJI: It's a spiral. It goes around in a circle like a life cycle.

SIOBHAN: Like a life cycle like we are now, sitting in a circle.

DAMIEN: Like a bird lays an egg. The egg hatches and becomes a bird that lays an egg. It starts over again.

As you might suspect, these children have had many conversations about life cycles in their science program. Also, they recently began a study of chicks and have an incubator with fertilized eggs in their classroom. It is natural for children to solidify meaning by forming connections among ideas they understand.

Next the teacher lays a strip of paper on the floor. The strip has been divided to show a row of twelve squares. She then uses a set of two-side color chips to make a repeating pattern. She puts down a chip with its yellow side up in the first square; she turns the next chip so that the red side shows. In all, she puts out four chips: yellow, red, yellow, red, then asks, "What comes next?"

DANIELLA: Yellow. *[The teacher then motions the student to add that color chip to the others.]*

TEACHER: WHAT WILL GO IN THE NEXT SQUARE?

BETH: Red. *[Red is added to the emerging AB pattern.]*

TEACHER: LET'S STOP FOR A SECOND. I WANT YOU TO PREDICT. WHAT WILL GO IN THE LAST SQUARE OF OUR STRIP?

DAMIEN: Let's find out. We can just put the chips down, yellow, red.

TEACHER: WAIT. I WANT EVERYONE TO MAKE A PREDICTION IN HIS OR HER OWN MIND. *[A long silence follows; some of the children try to position their bodies so that they can see the entire strip on the rug as they point in the air and mouth the words* red *and* yellow.*]*

TEACHER: DOES EVERYONE HAVE A PREDICTION READY? *[Heads nod in agreement.]* PUT YOUR THUMB UP IF YOU THINK IT WILL BE BLUE.

SIOBHAN: It can't be blue. There is *no* blue here.

TEACHER: HOW ABOUT YELLOW? *[Three or four thumbs go up.]*

TEACHER: HOW ABOUT RED? *[Many thumbs go up.]* HOW DO YOU KNOW?

ANITA: I went one at a time *[she points to the next empty square]* yellow, red, yellow, red. Each time you go to the next one.

KIMI: I went back to the beginning. Yellow, red, yellow, red . . .

MICHAEL: Sometimes squares are odd numbers. If it was even and started with yellow, it would end with red.

TEACHER: DOES EVERYONE FOLLOW MICHAEL?

HUNTER: Yeah, each square is a number. *[He motions to the squares as he counts aloud, one through twelve.]*

TEACHER: SO THERE ARE TWELVE SQUARES ON OUR STRIP OF PAPER. HOW DOES THAT HELP US KNOW WHAT COLOR GOES IN THE LAST SQUARE?

MICHAEL: It's hard to explain.

SARITA: If you had blue first, it wouldn't end with blue. It would go blue, green, blue, green.

KIMI: I think I understand. If you added one more it would end in yellow.

TEACHER: WHAT DO YOU MEAN?

KIMI: Odd would have yellow at the front and end.

ANITA: You can use the number to tell the color.

KEIJI: I did it both ways. I did it Anita's way and I did yellow, red, yellow, red.

TEACHER: DID YOU COUNT HOW MANY SQUARES?

KEIJI: Yes. I knew when to stop cause that's the end.

BENITA: One more is odd. All odds are yellow.

HUNTER: I don't agree with Benita. It could end in a different color. It doesn't have to end with yellow.

TEACHER: WE'VE BEEN SITTING AND TALKING FOR AWHILE. I WOULD LIKE EACH OF YOU TO GO BACK TO YOUR WORKSPACES AND TRY THIS CHALLENGE. WHAT IF WE ADDED MORE SQUARES TO OUR STRIP? WHAT COLOR WOULD GO IN SQUARE EIGHTEEN? YOU CAN BUILD, WRITE, DRAW, OR FIND SOME OTHER WAY TO FIGURE THAT OUT. THEN I WANT YOU TO SHOW HOW YOU THOUGHT ABOUT IT AND HOW YOU KNOW YOUR ANSWER IS CORRECT.

The children move to their workspaces. Damien collects a small tub of two-color chips along the way. He places the tub in the middle of the table where he is sitting and announces, "We can use these. You'll need about four. Oh, no, more than that." He takes a couple of large handfuls and begins to place the chips so that their color alternates from yellow to red. After working for a bit, he stops and counts softly. "I have fourteen in my pattern," he announces. He then places four additional chips, one at a time, counting on from fourteen as he does so.

For his recording, Damien draws eighteen small squares on his paper (counting as he draws each one) and uses crayons to show the alternating chips. Then, using his red crayon, he records "red," to indicate the color of the eighteenth chip. He shows his work to Anita, who is sitting beside him.

"Good," Anita responds. "Now, we have to write how we know."

"Oh yeah. I forgot," replies Damien. He then draws a large yellow hand and brings his work to show his teacher. "The last color is red," he announces as he shows her his paper.

"How did you know that?" she asks.

"Cause it's a pattern. I made it," he explains as he points to his picture of a hand.

Damien's work (see Figure 8–1), is typical of many young students. He merely continues the pattern, without thinking about the relationship between the colors and numerical positions of the chips.

Anita's work does show attention to numerical position (see Figure 8–2). As she represents each tile, she numbers it. Then she records (as translated from her invented spelling), "It still lands on red. Eighteen is an even number. If it starts on yellow it will end on red."

Hunter proceeds somewhat differently (see Figure 8–3). He draws only six tiles, counting on from the original pattern of twelve. He records the answer, red, and explains how he continued the pattern. His teacher sees his work and wonders if he will simply continue the pattern for a greater number as well. She asks, "What would be the last color if there were twenty squares?"

Hunter thinks for a bit and then replies, "Red. Ten and ten is twenty, so they each need ten."

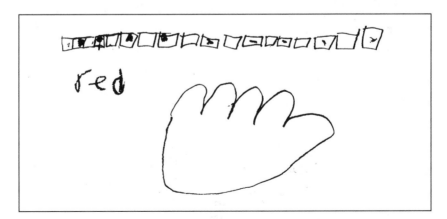

FIGURE 8–1   *Damien's work*

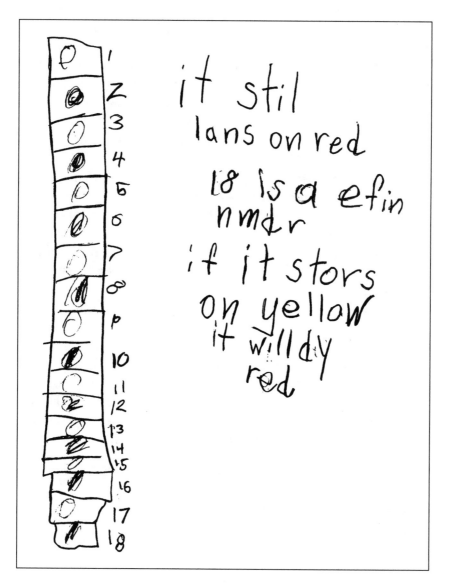

FIGURE 8–2   *Anita's work*

Joshua and Hilda are sitting together. While he works, Joshua turns to Hilda and says, "It will always be red if you have an even number of squares." Note that Joshua includes this comment on his recording, as well (see Figure 8–4).

Hilda replies, "That's true. Eight and ten are even numbers, too, and they are red."

FIGURE 8–3 *Hunter's work*

Joshua then adds, "If it's ten, it's even. You'll have five yellow and five reds."

The teacher is nearby and overhears this conversation. To extend their thinking, she asks about twenty squares.

"That's even, so it's red," explains Hilda.

"They'll be ten red and ten yellow," adds Joshua.

The teacher is impressed with their thinking and decides to challenge them further. "What about thirty-five?" she asks.

Joshua replies, "The last would be yellow, because five is an odd number."

Teacher Reflection

It's always exciting to me when the children begin to extend their understanding of patterns. I know that they can continue a simple pattern; they even have a sense that their patterns could go on forever. This is not insignificant, but I want them to experience the mathematical power of making a prediction, and knowing it's right, without having to place each chip, one at a time. In this way I believe I'm helping the children to develop algebraic ideas. When they begin to develop generalizations, I believe they are on their way.

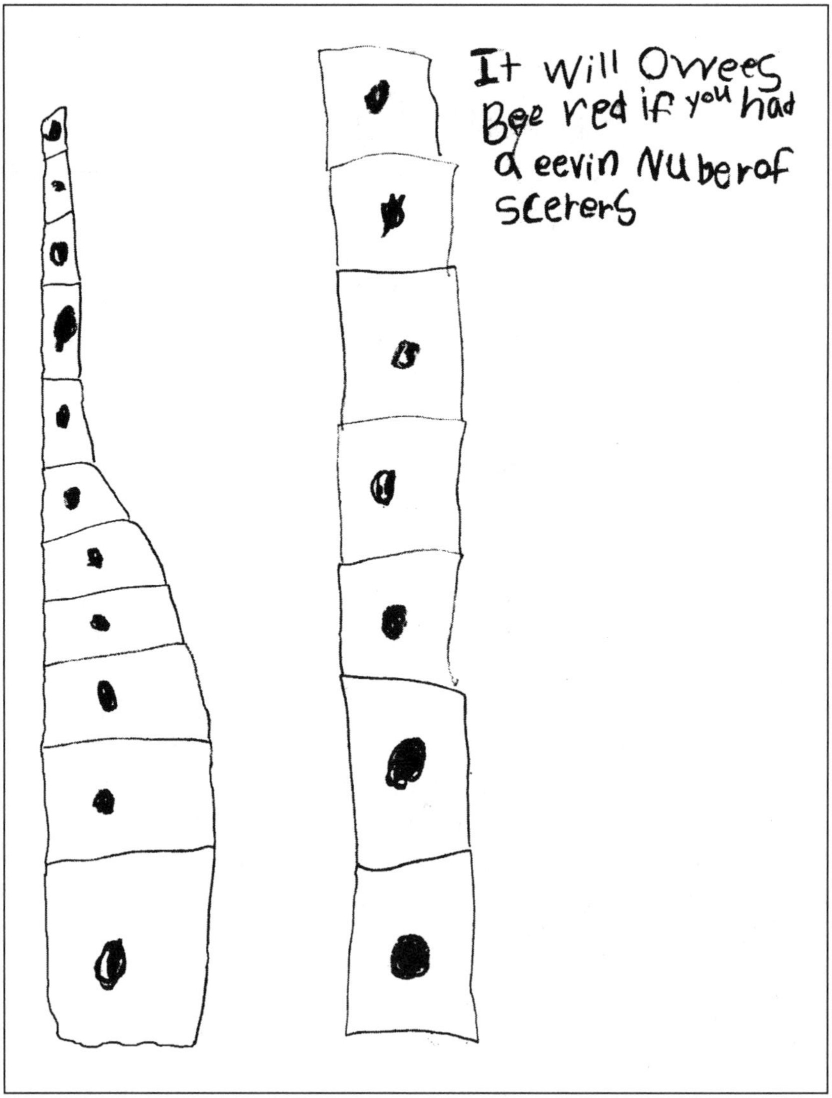
It will Owees Bee red if you had a eevin Nuberof scerers

FIGURE 8–4 *Joshua's work*

Michael's comment is telling. It is difficult for these young children to explain their understanding of patterns. Students often respond, "I just know it" or "Because it's a pattern" when I ask them how they know. But I still think it is important to probe further. I want them to begin to reflect on their thinking. Clearly not all of the students understood Michael's observation, but several, like Joshua and Hilda, built on his idea of the importance of whether or not there were an even or odd number of chips.

These first graders have ideas about even and odd numbers. They recognize that these numbers alternate. I was pleased to see them associate this aspect of number with this activity. Some children clearly made a connection between a number being even and being able to identify a "double sum" for that number. I was fascinated by the way Joshua identified 35 as odd. I'm fairly certain he doesn't know that you can identify a number as either even or odd by examining only the digit in the one's place, but rather, that he only attended to the five. But, it is a beginning.

When I offer my students time to consider a new idea as a whole group and then let them head off on their own to continue working on these new ideas, I am constantly amazed at how much they learn from one another. When Keiji talked about using "Anita's way," I beamed inside. I know these first graders are listening to each other and by trying on someone else's strategy they can expand their own pool of knowledge. Sometimes they take these ideas from our whole-group conversations; sometimes new ideas emerge when children work side by side. At some point I know a groundswell of ideas are burgeoning. On this day, I believe the whole conversation about odd and even numbers unfolded because one child's comment sparked an idea in another. I did not expect "odd and even" to be a driving force in the discussion. We've talked about odd and even numbers when we've counted the number of days in school. I was amazed to see these ideas come into play here. I expected to see use of the counting-all strategy and some counting-on strategies, but the odd and even work surprised me.

Not all children approached the work using ideas about odd and even numbers. Many continued to lay out the total number of elements in the pattern that I was asking them to consider. Whether they were counting all, counting on, or making some kind of generalization based on their ideas of odd and even numbers and how they relate to this AB pattern, all of the children were able to wrestle with these new ideas and formulate a response that was based on sound mathematics.

Growing Patterns

It is early spring and a kindergarten class is reading *Ten Black Dots* by Donald Crews during shared reading. This counting book provides young children with a wonderful set of illustrations from which they can form solid visual images about quantities, numerical patterns, and operations. As the final few pages are shared, children often make comments about the images, as witnessed in the following conversation. The children are focused on an illustration that looks like this:

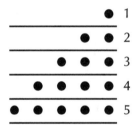

SAM: It looks like a triangle.

DEBBIE: It does, but it's a funny triangle. You could turn it around. *[Note preference for traditional positions of triangles.]*

CAROLINE: I see a square. *[She comes up to the book and draws her finger around all of the dots and lines on the left-hand page.]*

SCOTT: The numbers keep growing.

PAT: It looks like stairs.

TEACHER: SCOTT IS CORRECT, THE NUMBERS ARE GROWING; IN FACT, THIS TYPE OF PATTERN IS OFTEN CALLED A GROWING PATTERN.

While repeating patterns receive greater attention at this level, it is important to recognize that young children can recognize other types of patterns as well. Our system of counting is a growing pattern; the numbers increase (or decrease) by a constant difference of one. On the next page of the book, the numeric pattern continues, with 6 at the top and 10 at the bottom. This time the geometric formation of dots points to the right.

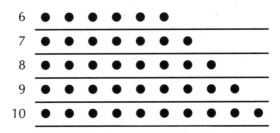

ISABELLA: I see a triangle. *[Note the incorrect identification of a triangular shape.]*

NORM: It looks like a shoe.

SHELLY: Or a slipper.

ALICE: It's the stairs and then the bedroom.

MYLES: Each time they have one more dot.

ALU: The line gets bigger.

EMMA: Longer. The line gets longer.

DAYTON: It's like you add one each time. Five and one is six; six and one is seven. The one is like the leader.

It is clear that the children react to these illustrations on very different levels. Some connect the geometric shapes formed by the dots to meaningful real-world objects. Others focus on the number of dots. Dayton builds on Scott's earlier notion that the numbers are growing. He explicitly recognizes an essential aspect of counting—that is, each number is one more than the number before and one less than the next number. To adults, this relationship is obvious, but for children, it is an important insight into how our numeration system works. Later, it can help them to write larger numbers and to easily add and subtract one from a given number.

By second grade, students can explore more complex growing patterns. In May, one teacher decides to explore such patterns with her students for the first time. Throughout the year, her students have used manipulatives to explore repeating patterns, and they have looked for patterns on their classroom calendar. The children have become adept at seeing patterns in the hundreds chart in counting by 1s, 10s, 2s, and 5s. By observing their work, the teacher has become confident that the students have a firm grasp on these types of patterns and now feels that they are ready for a greater challenge.

To begin, she asks her students to look at a pattern (see Figure 8–5) she made with an oversized set of pattern blocks. Her students are familiar with working with pattern blocks, and she thinks that this familiarity will help them to take the next step. Like many of their math discussions, she starts by asking, "What do you notice?"

JEREMY: It kind of looks like two arrows.

ANDREA: You're adding one at a time. There's one, and then there's two.

TEACHER: WATCH CAREFULLY, I'M GOING TO ADD A NEW PART. [*The teacher adds three squares with six triangles; see Figure 8–6.*]

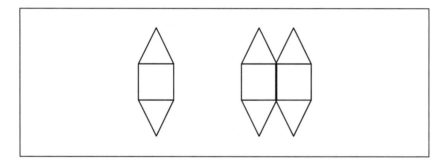

FIGURE 8–5   *The initial pattern*

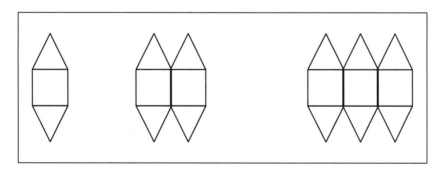

FIGURE 8–6   *The expanded pattern*

ELLA: There's one, then there's two. Then one, two, three squares. Then you put three triangles.

ANDREA: No, six.

BESTOR: Six because you put three on the top and three on the bottom.

CHARLIE: If you pushed it all together it would look like a caterpillar with green legs.

AGGIE: If you took the triangles off the bottom it would look like houses.

LEXIA: If you folded it over it would be the same on both sides. What's that called again?

CHARLIE: Symmetry.

TEACHER: WHAT PART SHOULD I PUT DOWN NEXT TO CONTINUE MY PATTERN?

THEO: Four, because it's one, two, three already.

TEACHER: FOUR WHAT?

THEO: Squares.

BESTOR: It's four arrows.

TEACHER: WHAT DO YOU MEAN?

BESTOR: You can count the whole arrow and have four or just the squares in the middle and get four.

TEACHER: SO HOW DO YOU KNOW?

JEREMY: When you look at those, it's like one, then one more.

TEACHER: WHAT ARE YOU COUNTING?

ANDREA: The triangles are counting by twos, the squares are counting by ones.

TEACHER: WHAT DO YOU MEAN, THE TRIANGLES ARE COUNTING BY TWOS?

ANDREA: See, you need eight [moving to put the triangles in place with the four squares that have already been placed on the rug].

SARITA: One plus one is two, two plus two is four, three plus three is six [pointing to the triangles in each part of the pattern as she speaks]. Now four plus four is eight. Then you need five plus five is ten.

CAMILLE: One, two, one, two is a pattern.

LEXIA: But this pattern doesn't go like that. This one is getting bigger.

TEACHER: WHAT DO YOU MEAN?

LEXIA: Each time the arrows get bigger. See, one, then two, then three, then four [pointing to each element of the growing pattern].

ANDREA: It's an adding pattern. You add one more each time.

SARITA: Sometimes you add two more, like the triangles.

TEACHER: LEXIA SAYS, "THIS PATTERN IS GETTING BIGGER." ANDREA SAYS IT'S AN "ADDING PATTERN." WHAT DO OTHER PEOPLE THINK?

BRYCE: It does get bigger. Each time you add more.

LINCOLN: They are both right. I agree with Bryce.

CARLINA: It can keep going like with the other kind of patterns we do.

TEACHER: IS THIS LIKE THE OTHER KIND OF PATTERNS WE'VE WORKED WITH?

CARLINA: No—they repeat, this doesn't. It gets bigger.

TEACHER: WE HAVE BEEN SAYING THAT THIS PATTERN GETS BIGGER OR THAT WE CAN ADD ON TO THE PATTERN. SOMETIMES PEOPLE CALL THESE "GROWING PATTERNS." IF WE WANT TO ADD THE NEXT FIGURE TO THE PATTERN, WHAT WILL IT LOOK LIKE?

JEREMY: The next one will have five squares.

SARITA: And ten triangles [adding quickly].

TEACHER: CAN YOU PREDICT THE NUMBER OF TRIANGLES THE FIGURE IN THE PATTERN WILL HAVE IF IT HAS EIGHT SQUARES?

PAVEL: That's easy. Eight and eight is sixteen.

TEACHER: DO YOU AGREE WITH PAVEL? [Several heads nod.] WHY?

RICKI: Because you need them for the top and the bottom.

TEACHER: WHAT CAN YOU DO TO MAKE SURE?

RICKI: We can make it. Look. [Ricki makes the figure and counts the sixteen triangles.]

TEACHER: CAN YOU MAKE A PREDICTION OF HOW MANY SQUARES THE PATTERN WILL HAVE IF IT HAS FOURTEEN TRIANGLES?

CARLINA: Fourteen plus fourteen is . . .

BESTOR: No, that's too many. There are less squares than triangles.

CHARLIE: Yeah, it would be seven, because seven plus seven is fourteen. On every square, you need a triangle on each side. So seven on one side and seven on the other.

TEACHER: IS THERE ANOTHER WAY YOU CAN BE SURE?

CAMILLE: We could put them out.

TEACHER: BEFORE WE PUT OUT MORE PIECES, LET'S THINK ABOUT THIS. IF YOU HAVE FOURTEEN TRIANGLES, HOW MANY SQUARES WILL YOU NEED?

SARITA: Charlie is right, it's seven. When there is one square, one plus one is two and you have two triangles, one on each side. When you have two squares, it's two plus two is four. So I think seven plus seven is fourteen and you need seven squares.

LEXIA: I can count like this, too [pointing to the first element in the pattern]. Two [splitting her fingers to point to each triangle], four [repeating this same motion with the next element], six, eight, ten, twelve [pointing to the next elements], fourteen [pointing to the next empty space, as though another element was on the ground in front of her].

TEACHER: WHAT ABOUT TWENTY-TWO TRIANGLES? HOW MANY SQUARES WOULD THERE BE?

THEO: Seventeen.

CARLINA: Eleven.

SASHA: Eleven—I know five and five is ten, and one more would be eleven.

LEXIA: I know eleven plus eleven is twenty-two. I know eleven on top and eleven on the bottom. I'm born on December twenty-second, so I know eleven plus eleven is twenty-two.

These second graders are clearly capable of having a rich and long conversation about this growing pattern. Note that in the early stage of their conversation, Jeremy refers to arrows, Charlie suggests the similarity of the third figure to a caterpillar, and Aggie notes that the figures would look like houses without the bottom row of triangles. Lexia makes a connection to a mathematical idea, symmetry. These comments illustrate ways in which the children attempt to make sense of what they see. They are connecting these figures to ideas with which they are already familiar. By sharing these observations, they offer other children a way to think about the figures.

Note that the teacher began by merely asking students what they noticed. She then asked them to watch her make the next figure, so that they could gain a visual image of it being formed. Next, she asked students to predict the fourth and fifth figures in the pattern. It is important that the children continue the pattern before they make more complex conjectures. As these next figures are formed, the conversation focuses on how this pattern is different from the repeating patterns with which the children are familiar. By contrasting these two types of patterns, they are able to clarify their new ideas about growing patterns.

Within this pattern, the number of squares and triangles vary. As the children form the next figures and further discuss the pattern, they begin to discover the relationship between the numbers of squares and triangles. Relating the change in one variable (number of squares) to the change in another variable (number of triangles) is an important algebraic idea. Students are discovering a functional relationship within this simple pattern. They are developing mathematically powerful ideas that can be used to determine what other figures will look like without continuing the pattern, element by element. Significantly, some children are able to make predictions both from squares to triangles and from triangles to squares.

The teacher is impressed with the children's understanding and interest. However, she is aware that not all of the children contributed to the discussion, and she wants to offer everyone a chance to work with these ideas. Thus, she is ready with a new task for all to tackle. This time, the children are given a different growing pattern with specific directions (see Figure 8–7).

For the most part, everyone works independently at first. It is interesting to note that only a few students use pattern blocks to aid their thinking. It is important, however, to have "real" materials available at all times and to encourage their use. Even children who don't think that they need materials will sometimes seek them out when their ideas feel uncertain.

Comments are exchanged with neighbors as children become familiar with the pattern; most comments involve comparisons between this pattern and the one just explored.

Charlie observes, "This one is different. It has more squares."

"This one is getting taller; the other one was getting bigger," adds Theo.

Lexia focuses on the fact that both are growing patterns, commenting, "It still adds on, going up." She records several specific observations about the pattern (Figure 8–8). Note that she

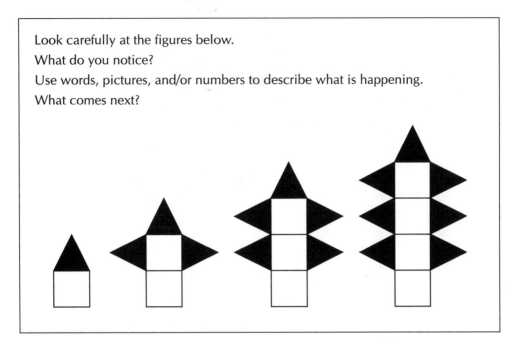

Look carefully at the figures below.

What do you notice?

Use words, pictures, and/or numbers to describe what is happening.

What comes next?

FIGURE 8–7 *The new growing pattern and directions*

begins by indicating the aspects of the figures that remain constant—the lack of triangles on the bottom and the single triangle at the top. She then specifies how the figures change from one to the next, the addition of a square with a triangle on either side. Finally, she draws the next figure correctly.

While Jenna does not indicate what the next figure will be, she makes several important observations. She compares each figure to the one that comes next and notes that one square and two triangles are added each time. She records the number of squares and triangles in each figure (see Figure 8–9, page 205). Though she has recorded the number of triangles in the fourth figure incorrectly, looking for patterns within parts of the figure can be a powerful problem-solving strategy. She also indicates that the first figure looks like a house; the second, a clown; the third, a rocket ship; and the fourth, a cactus growing in the desert.

After the children complete this problem, their teacher has a follow-up set of questions for them to tackle. As she knows that her students work at different levels, she has written each question on a separate, short piece of paper. This way, she can hand

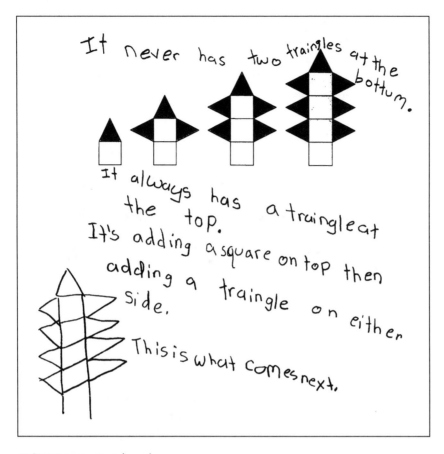

It never has two traingles at the bottom.

It always has a traingle at the top.

It's adding a square on top then adding a traingle on either side.

This is what comes next.

FIGURE 8–8   *Lexia's work*

the questions to the students one at a time. Thus, students can explore a common problem while focusing on those questions that are developmentally appropriate.

The first question is, "How will the next figure look? How do you know?" All of the children are able to draw or build the fifth figure in the pattern correctly. In their own ways, their explanations indicate that they have used the first four figures and what they know about the pattern to identify the next element. Carlina's explanation focuses on the growing nature of the pattern as she writes, "I know because it keeps on adding." Sarita records, "other paper," as a way to refer to the drawing of the first four figures in the pattern. Sasha explains, "Because you just add a square and two triangles." Charlie uses a picture to illustrate his thinking.

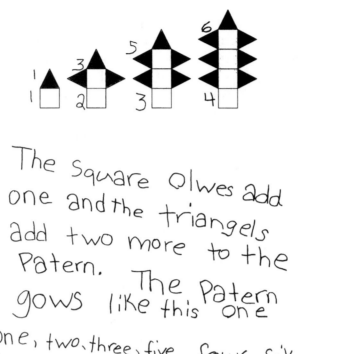

The square olwes add one and the triangels add two more to the Patern. The Patern gows like this one

one, two, three, five, four, six. the first one looks likea house the secont one looks like a cown the therd one looks like a rockit ship and the forth one looks like a growing cacktis in the desert.

FIGURE 8-9 *Jenna's work*

He first draws the fourth figure, then he draws the fifth one right beside it. "It just keeps going," he explains to his teacher.

The next question posed skips the sixth figure in the pattern and asks, "How many triangles will there be in the figure with seven squares?" Almost all of the children are able to respond in some manner. Most draw seven squares, add the appropriate triangles, and then count them. Three students add triangles to the bottom square as well, and thus get an incorrect answer. Few students provide explanations, although Charlie (see Figure 8–10) indicates how he counted. When asked about his work, he explained, "Six and six is twelve and one more on top is thirteen." Note that he wrote 7 + 7, and did not correct this recording or respond to this conflict in any way.

A couple of children are able to find the answer without making a drawing or using the pattern blocks. Carlina relies on what she knows about the pattern. She explains, "Well, I know at the end there won't be any triangles. So it would be six. Six plus six equals twelve; one plus twelve equals thirteen." She then circles the 13, presumably to indicate that it is the answer.

Jeremy refers to the relationship between the number of squares and the number of triangles in the previous figures. In his own way (see Figure 8–11) he indicates that there were four more triangles than squares in the figure with five squares and predicts five more triangles than squares in the figure with six squares, and six more triangles than squares in the figure with seven squares. He adds the seven (number of squares) and six (number of more triangles than squares). He announces, "thirteen triangles," and then draws the figure to check his prediction.

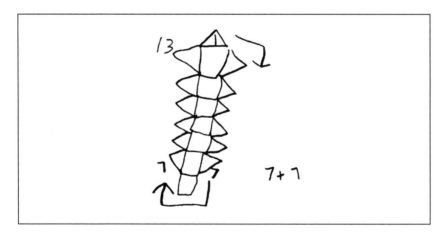

FIGURE 8–10   *Charlie's work*

FIGURE 8–11   *Jeremy's work*

Only about half of the children are asked to make a generalization by responding to the question, "How can you find the number of triangles when you know the number of squares?" Many students reply by choosing a number of squares, say eight, and showing how to find the number of triangles for that number of squares.

Carlina attempts a generalization (see Figure 8–12): "Well you take the square at the bottom off. Then you plus the number of squares you had with the same number." Although she neglects to add one to account for the triangle at the top, she is able to articulate significant generalizations about the relationship between triangles and squares.

Sarita records the following succinct generalization: "add squares – 1." When her teacher asks about this idea, Sarita replies, "Say there's nine squares. Then nine plus nine is eighteen and eighteen minus one is seventeen." After listening to this explanation her teacher asks, "How did you discover this?"

"I looked at the numbers," explains Sarita. She apparently found a relationship between the number of squares and the number of triangles, which allowed her to predict the number of triangles, given the number of squares, without thinking about their actual arrangements in the figures. By focusing on the

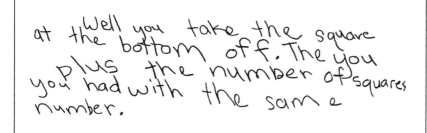

FIGURE 8–12 *Carlina's generalization*

numerical relationships, without regard for the physical place-ments of the figures, she worked in much the same way as chil-dren might when playing a game of Guess My Rule (another way to explore patterns and functions). In this game, students find a numerical relationship or rule that allows them to connect the numbers in the first column to the numbers in the second col-umn. There is no corresponding visual image.

In contrast, Sasha's correct generalization relies heavily on the physical models. He explains, "You see how many squares you have. For every square you have two triangles on the side except for the bottom. Don't forget the one on top."

Over the course of the next couple of days, the children explore several additional growing patterns. Then they are pre-sented with the task of creating and explaining their own patterns. After a few false starts, Lexia creates a pattern that satisfies her (see Figure 8–13). Note that there is a growing and a repeating pattern embedded in her figures. Lexia demonstrates clearly that she knows the differences between these two types of patterns.

Teacher Reflection

I think my students are brilliant. I am so thrilled with the way they tackled this brief excursion with growing patterns. I was pretty sure they were ready for this as we have worked with repeating patterns so much, but I wasn't sure how far to take them. A colleague had sug-gested the idea of having additional work on small pieces of paper so that I could hand a printed problem

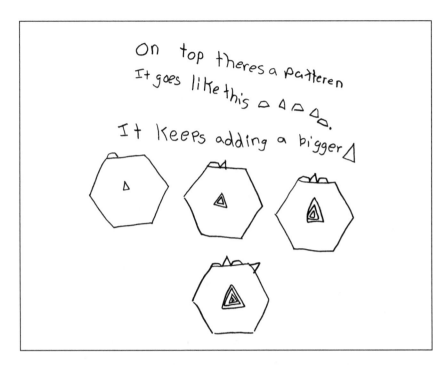

On top theres a patteren
It goes like this △ △ △ △.
It keeps adding a bigger △

FIGURE 8–13 *Lexia's pattern*

or question to each child, as they were ready to take on new challenges. This worked well to keep everyone moving in their own zone or level of comfort.

I find the range of strategies fascinating. I made the pattern blocks readily available, though I often find it interesting to see who reaches for them in moments like this. For the most part children are able to monitor their own need to use manipulatives. Some think that they aren't as smart if they use them. I try to meet this head-on and use the blocks as often as possible to model my own thinking. At the same time, I know that when I hand something out on paper, most if not all children begin by drawing or writing ideas. I often wonder if this is too hard for some children, but they do rise to the occasion. I still struggle to define my expectations about representing complex ideas on paper.

I want to make sure I always have time to talk to children about their work. Charlie's work confused me [see Figure 8–10]. I wanted to hear what he had to say about his work. When he so quickly told me six plus six is twelve and one more is thirteen, I wondered how that thinking related to what he wrote. He did not offer any new insights and I did not have time to probe further. I also know that when I stick too long with one student, I can erode their confidence. Charlie was beaming about his work. I decided to follow up at another point with a similar problem.

As I present a new problem to my students I want to give them ample time to digest the ideas. I find it interesting that we can go from a whole-group conversation that is buzzing with ideas, to total silence when children shift to "working on their own." I do not say that they need to work independently, but I've noticed that when I hand out a problem on paper, there is always a few moments of silence. Then, as children begin to dissect what is being asked, they naturally begin to talk in pairs. These conversations ebb and flow throughout the work session. I know that these moments are powerful. Children do see each other as resources or sounding boards. Sometimes I notice that children share ideas or ask questions when no one is listening. This feels so real. Adults, too, often think out loud. The children use the vocalization as a way to sort something out on their own.

The range of strategies for solving the problem and for representing thinking is so great. When I listen to Sarita develop a conjecture about number of squares and triangles by using two examples as the basis for her theory, I am delighted. She says, "When there is one square, one plus one is two and you have two triangles. When you have two squares, it's two plus two equals four. So I think seven plus seven is fourteen . . ." When Sarita adds, "So I think . . ." to her explanation, I hear her saying "this is my theory." She has agreed with Charlie's response and acknowledges this, and then adds her own thinking. It is in the formulization of her theory that I see algebraic ideas at work.

Right after that, Lexia talked about how she counted the same triangles and squares to get the same answer but she did so in a different way. This is so exciting to me. Where did these ideas come from? How do I continue to support my students and their pursuits in mathematics over time so this can continue to happen for all children? I believe having a solid sense of my goals along with time to allow students to wrestle with these ideas so that they can formulate their own theories is so important. I also believe this happens best when children learn from one another. Learning to share ideas by engaging in conversations, building or drawing examples to support one's thinking, and being encouraged to share ideas with others are important steps to building confidence and deeper understanding even in new territory like early algebraic thinking.

9

Seeing and Hearing

The conversations and representations that kindergarten, first-, and second-grade students generate when working with mathematical ideas permeate this book. Their voices sing out with questions, misunderstandings, strategies, and solutions. Coupled with their elegant representations, their thinking about mathematics is inspiring. Their insights are keen. They demonstrate a great deal of understanding in each of the content strands explored.

The teachers portrayed herein add their own perceptive comments, questions, personal doubts, and professional triumphs to the voices of the children. The Teacher Reflections shed much light on the purposes and practices of show-and-tell in K–2 mathematics instruction. The comments and queries made by teachers in the classroom vignettes illustrate the power of decisions that teachers make on a daily basis. It is clear that these teachers do not take the responsibilities of teaching lightly.

When teachers train their eyes and ears to see and hear what children show and tell about their individual and collective mathematical ideas, they gain a better understanding of the developmental and cognitive needs of their students. They gain a better appreciation for the mathematics that they themselves must know to work successfully with young students. They begin to recognize important milestones in the learning process. They also begin to ask questions about how to best guide students' thinking, questions such as, "When should models be offered?" and "When should additional explanations be required of students?"

These questions are legitimate and demand responses. In today's high-stakes educational arena, we need to work together, to assist each other in our inquiries about teaching and learning. It is not just one teacher or researcher who holds the key, but our collective wisdom that can yield the most enlightening insights into the artful practice of teaching.

In this spirit, what follows are a few of the questions teachers most commonly ask about the show-and-tell process. These questions, and the responses that accompany them, are meant to help all of us better support young children in their pursuit of mathematical knowledge.

What Is the Purpose of a Representation?

Through the examples in this book and in the work that we observe in our own classrooms, we see clearly that representations take on a variety of configurations and purposes. Simultaneously, they may serve as a way to think about a problem, to tell how a solution was found, and to communicate an answer. This is the beauty of a representation; it is both a process and a product. It serves as a sense-making vehicle while a student is immersed in a problem, but later provides a product that can stimulate student sharing and guide teacher decision making.

Representations that show how students solved a problem have many purposes. It is unlikely that young children would be able to share their thinking with their peers without such artifacts to trigger their memories. They help students to be clear about their ideas, and thus to consider the similar or contradictory ideas of others. They give teachers insight into student thinking and allow for the detection of procedural errors and misconceptions. They provide a record that can be compared to later work in order to note differences and growth.

As it takes a great deal of time and work for students to create these representations, students need to understand why making them is so important. Here's one teacher's thinking about how to help students understand the importance of representing their thinking processes.

Teacher Reflection

Sometimes the children in my class wince at the thought of adding more to their work. They give me that suspicious or frustrated look when I ask them to show how they know something, or to show another way of doing something. I have tried to set up a reasonable expectation for why we do this. I want them to understand why it is important for them to communicate their ideas to others.

Communication is a vital skill. To reinforce its importance, I might say something like, "Even if I didn't have a conversation with you, from your recording I can see how you were thinking about solving the problem." My hope is for them to see a purpose for sharing their ideas with others, and that their work provides them with a record of the steps they took. This is an important and complex metacognitive process. I know it is hard for these six-, seven-, and eight-year-olds to think about their own thinking, but I believe they are capable of doing so.

Is One Form of Representation Better Than Another?

We need to remind ourselves that representations come in many forms. They can be drawings or the manipulation of objects. They may include lengthy written descriptions, an equation, or just a numeral. They may involve dramatization or pantomime. We need to open ourselves to a myriad of formats.

We also need to remind ourselves that representations have always played a vital role in mathematics. There are many conventional forms of representation to which children need exposure. Most representations are not newly invented. The conventional use of an equation such as $16 - 9 = 7$, is a useful and efficient representation, *once the child understands its meaning*.

A powerful tool for developing that understanding is to have children actively engaged in making their own representations and then making the connections between invented and conventional forms. As highlighted in the following teacher remarks, ideally, representations are efficient as well as personally meaningful.

Teacher Reflection

I have often noticed my students recording representations that do not reflect the actual steps they have taken. I wonder why this happens. Is it too difficult for them to record their processes? Are they adding a detailed drawing because they think that is what I want to see, or because they like to draw? Do they write an equation because they see a friend has done so, because it has meaning for them, or because they believe there is an expectation to do so?

I want my students to learn effective and efficient ways to represent their ideas. Yet at the same time, I don't want this to be a contest or some unspoken game about giving me what they think I want to see. I want my first graders to see that the representations are for *them*. Yes, I want to understand the representations, but, first and foremost, they should be records of the children's thinking: their ideas, their strategies, and their solutions.

If a Child Can Tell and Model with Manipulative Materials, Why Must They Draw and/or Write as Well?

Sometimes, when we try something new and find it effective, we over-generalize its use. We must be mindful of variation in supporting teaching and learning in our individual classrooms. It may be adequate, or even exemplary, if a child can model his thinking with manipulative materials. On the other hand, it may be cause for concern. Is the student resisting a paper-and-pencil activity? If so, why?

The goals of the show-and-tell approach are for children to communicate the mathematics that they understand and to deepen their mathematical ideas. If the child and teacher are satisfied that these goals have been reached, requiring more than one method of communication may not be necessary.

Further, it is not assumed that there is a hierarchy of methods of communication, but rather that different methods can support learning in different ways. There are times when a teacher may require students to try different strategies. Sometimes having a record on paper is easier to manage and respond to later. It is also important to provide practice using different strategies so that students can become familiar and comfortable with a variety of representational formats.

However, assignments that require a student to model *and* to draw *and* to write both numbers and words can become cumbersome and undermine the students' focus. Energy is spent on making sure they have met each requirement instead of on understanding the mathematics. Sometimes, too much time and energy is shifted into "teaching" and having students practice how to represent thinking, without regard for deepening that thinking.

What Happens When All My Students Want to Do Is Draw?

Kindergarten, first-, and second-grade students love to draw, and the development of creative expression is important at this age. Drawing is an easy way for young children to begin making mathematical representations on paper.

Many children add a great deal of detail to their drawings. Over time, it is important to help children make decisions about whether their chosen form of representation is effective and efficient. At some point, most children do seem to understand that their representations need not include irrelevant details. For example, they learn that apples can be represented using simple red circles. It is our role as teachers to help guide children to this point.

Moving from pictures to more abstract symbols and ultimately to numbers and equations is an important goal of elementary mathematics. We want our students to understand the symbolic nature of mathematics and to use this powerful tool with great command. But we must also remember that drawing is a useful aid and should remain among our students' strategies. In fact, adults often use drawing or diagrams to make sense of new information.

Do Students Always Have to Explain or Show Their Thinking?

Sometimes children respond to the persistent question "How do you know?" by saying, "I just know!" In our efforts to bring show and tell into the classroom, teachers are often frustrated by this response. Instead of accepting it as genuine, we question if the child actually understands the material. Yet, if adults were asked how they know what five plus five is, they might also respond, "I just know."

One of the goals of mathematics education is to help students internalize mathematical concepts and facts. If they respond, "I just know," might they sometimes be telling us that they have internalized this idea? As teachers, we must continue to examine this question. As powerful as show-and-tell approaches are, they must not be seen as ends in and of themselves. While students should be encouraged to explain their thinking, sometimes it is enough to simply accept that they just know.

Should Students Have to Show or Tell More Than One Way to Solve a Problem?

Knowing more than one way to think about or to solve a problem is powerful. For example, as shown in Chapter 4, there are a variety of strategies for finding sums. Being familiar and comfortable with several approaches allows us to choose the best approach for any particular example or circumstance. Occasionally requiring students to show two ways to find a sum helps children to develop and think about alternative techniques. However, always requiring a student to provide two solution methods can be tedious and result in negative attitudes.

As has been illustrated throughout this book, questions such as "Is there more you can tell me?" or "Is there something else you could show?" can lead to amazing outcomes. Students who appeared to be finished developed new insights and ideas; teachers gleaned new appreciation for their students' thinking. Yet, there are times when asking for more suggests that the existing work is not satisfactory. Over time, as we get to know our students better, we can learn when to expect more and when to move on.

Will the Representations My Students Record Change Over Time?

As students' representations are linked to their mathematical understandings, it is reasonable to expect changes over time. As can be seen in the K–2 examples included in this book, in general, second-grade work looks very different from kindergarten work. Sometimes these changes are dramatic; sometimes they are subtle.

Most students begin with simple drawings. Over time, the drawings may include written explanations; invented code; and conventional mathematical symbols, expressions, or equations. Representations may also begin to show more than one solution or more than one way to arrive at that solution. The mathematical knowledge demonstrated might be deeper, and connections may be made to other mathematical problems or ideas. Technical skills may change as well; for example, letters and numbers might be written more uniformly and there may be fewer letter/number reversals.

These changes do not all occur along a straight path or on a predictable timetable. Sometimes, when learning a new skill or concept, it appears as if students move back and forth, knowing something one day and not knowing it next. The following teacher contemplation addresses this notion of change over time.

Teacher Reflection

I used to send all of the student work home, that same day, if possible, but certainly by the next day. I wanted parents to know what was happening in my classroom. This was particularly easy when I first began teaching and relied heavily on a math workbook with perforated pages that could be torn out when completed.

When I started presenting only one problem on a piece of paper and students began to show such interesting responses, I was more reluctant to let the work go. I began to keep the work in folders and return it at the end of the unit. I bought a date stamp so that students could easily keep track of each piece. While it took time for parents to adjust to this approach, they grew more comfortable with it when they, too, got to see all of the work together.

By holding onto the work somewhat longer, I began to pay closer attention to the changes in the children's representations. These changes captured my interest, and I decided to give one problem several times over the course of the year. I chose a "How many of each?" type problem, where students are encouraged to find all the combinations of, for example, eight. By changing the problem setting and the total number, my students were able to explore the problem about six times.

It was amazing to see the variation of responses. Some children seemed to improve a bit each time they did one of these problems. Some children seemed to work the same way through two or three exposures to this problem type and then suddenly show dramatic growth. Sometimes a child would show change from one problem to the next—for example, by using numbers instead of drawings, and then the next time, revert to drawings. I really learned to appreciate the different pathways to learning.

I continue to use these problems every year. It has been a powerful way for me, the children, and the parents to better understand mathematical growth.

How Do I Best Support the Show-and-Tell Approach When Students Appear Stuck?

Support comes in many forms. It may come from asking a probing question, from making a suggestion to work with a partner, from having particular manipulative materials clearly available, by bringing the class back together because there are common misunderstandings, and occasionally, by demonstrating an approach.

Sometimes the best course of action is not to intervene at all. Some children just need more time to think, and will, on their own, arrive at new approaches within a few minutes. Some children may need additional or alternative learning opportunities over time. When a child is not ready to become "unstuck," probing questions may result in lost confidence or a reluctance to share ideas at a later point. Sometimes, we just need to accept a child's thinking at that moment. Support also comes from acknowledging the interests and ideas of individual children and establishing a safe environment where learning can happen.

Children may also appear stuck when they rely almost exclusively on one form of representation. We need to help them see other possibilities and to expand their repertoire of procedures. For example, a teacher may systematically choose to assign work that requires a child to use words or numbers, and discourages the use of drawings. If a need for these restrictions arises, we need to think about why we are setting limits. Is the child's limited use of representational forms hindering mathematical growth? How?

What Happens When a Conversation or Representation Creates Controversy?

When teachers were the "givers of mathematical truth," there was no room for mathematical controversies to arise. As children explore mathematical ideas from a more open perspective, however, controversies or conflicts occur naturally. Comments such as, "You can't do that" or "That's not right" are not uncommon.

During these moments we need to keep several things in mind. How do we help children talk to each other with respect? How do we help them listen and learn from one another? What should we do when something that is mathematically correct, but developmentally out of the reach of many students, gets shared?

It is important to remember that these moments offer rich opportunities for mathematical engagement. Questions such as "How can we decide?" or "Is there anything you could do to try to convince one another?" help to build a culture in which mathematical reasoning is the basis for decision making. In this way, these "controversies" build fertile ground for later exploration of mathematical proof.

How Much Should I Model for My Students?

Modeling is a critical teaching technique. It is a challenge, however, to show our students a possible approach without leading them to believe that this is the only way to proceed. We need to think critically about how, when, and how much we are going to model a strategy or method of representation. The following teacher reflection presents an example of this dilemma in a kindergarten classroom.

Teacher Reflection

Sometimes it is so difficult to know when to show children how they might do something. This morning my students were solving a problem about seven snowpeople with two arms each. They were trying to determine the total number of arms. When I approached Evan, I noticed that his paper was blank, there were no manipulative materials in sight, and he was counting his own fingers over and over again. I watched for a bit and noted that he didn't seem to be making any headway. I could tell that his frustration level was growing. Evan is a child who has some difficulty with self-control; outbursts are not uncommon.

I asked what he was doing and he replied, "I keep forgetting the number." To another child I might have responded, "Is there anything you can do to help you remember?" In this case, however, I felt as if more guidance was needed. I asked if he would like to work together a bit and he agreed. I then offered to draw lines as he counted.

He counted, "one, two," while touching two fingers at once, and I drew two parallel lines closely together. He then repeated the same motion while saying, "three, four," and again, I drew two lines. At that point I stopped and asked Evan to tell me what he saw in the drawing. He replied that there were two snowpeople and four arms. I then left Evan to complete the problem on his own and he was able to do so successfully.

I'm always a bit nervous about being "directive," but I felt Evan needed help in order to proceed with his mathematical thinking. Once he told me what the drawing meant, I was comfortable that he could use it successfully. Tomorrow I will give Evan another problem, maybe about the number of balls of snow needed to make six snowpeople. I wonder if he will remember that it helps to make a drawing of some sort to keep track. If he does, I wonder if he will continue to use lines. Perhaps he will use a circle to remind him of the snowballs.

How Do I Start Debriefing Sessions?

When a class comes together to set up a new problem or to debrief one that has been considered, many voices and possibilities need to be recognized. Some teachers begin by having their students share in a round-robin type fashion. Each child gets a brief moment to share a thought, question, or technique. This often happens after the answer to a problem has been agreed upon so that the focus is not on the actual solution, but rather on the ways students arrived at that solution. For this to happen, teachers first need to be sure that there is a high level of agreement about the solution.

Sometimes teachers make some prior decisions about who is going to share. By scanning the overall class, a teacher may see that a new strategy has emerged or that a review of some type of method might be helpful. Sometimes students speak by showing their recordings to their classmates and sometimes the teacher acts as a scribe by writing or drawing on chart paper, an overhead, or the chalkboard so that all can see.

When leading these discussions, our role is that of facilitator. We need to help the students keep the conversation going by asking probing questions and seeking further ideas. It is a subtle and artful form of teaching. It is tempting at times to want to "instruct" by reacting to each comment every child makes. Even the most seasoned teachers struggle with knowing when to intervene and when to observe. We need to recognize that this is a dramatic shift in our roles and be patient as we learn.

How Do I Organize and Keep Track of the Work and Information I Collect from My Students?

Anecdotal records are now commonplace in K–2 classrooms. Having a clipboard or notepad available during math time to record conversations that we overhear is very helpful. It is not possible, or necessary, to write every word. Even a simple notation can help jog our memories when we are planning for future instruction, preparing for conferences or report cards, or sharing our practice with colleagues.

The tangible artifacts students generate with manipulative materials can be captured with a camera. Many teachers ask their students to keep written work in math journals or to collect single sheets or prepared packets in a folder. It is important to keep some pieces or copies of work in order to look for growth over time. It is also important to send completed work home with students so that families (including caregivers) can monitor growth as well, and offer praise for a job well done. Families need to be in the show-and-tell loop, too.

Why and When Should I Write on a Child's Paper?

There are many reasons why we write on a child's paper. Sometimes we need to facilitate the representation by acting as a recorder. We want to keep the mathematical momentum going. If a child is restricted because he or she has trouble writing, we can temporarily become their hands and record what they say. Other times, we may want to record something that they have said for our own purposes. Placing the comments in quotes can help us recall that these are the student's words. When recording a conversation between teacher and child, some teachers put the child's words in quotes and identify what the teacher says or asks using a marginal notation, such as a T with a circle around it. In this way we can create something similar to a Running Record in reading. For the purpose of assessment, we want to capture as much of the authentic interaction as possible.

Written comments or symbols can also be added to a student's work once the student has submitted it. Many teachers have developed efficient systems for responding to student work. They know that there are different audiences for these responses. First and foremost these remarks are for the student. Later, when work goes home or is shared in a conference or portfolio, they are for a parent or family member. The comments also help teachers to remember a particular aspect of the work or the child's thinking.

Teacher Reflection

Over the years I have struggled with what to write on a child's paper. I want to comment on their progress, validate their effort, and keep the focus on the math. But I run out of time after school, when I also have reading logs and writing journals that beg for responses. Fortunately, my current system is working well.

My first goal is to try and respond to work with the child present. I know this is not always possible, but I've found that immediate feedback is the best. I've refined my system to include two symbols—a simple smiley face or a small circle or O. The students and their families have come to recognize that a smiley face on the paper means I've looked carefully at the work, I agree with the answer(s), and understand the representation(s). If I place a circle next to a response it means to "look again." When work is passed back, children know to focus their attention on this part of the work or answer. I might also include a request such as "Can you say more about your thinking?" I try to form things in a question so that it acts as an invitation to continue the work and not as a punitive statement of rejection. I use this system if I'm checking work alone or with a child by my side. Once a child shows me any revisions of the work, I can easily add a K to the O, and the paper then reads "OK"! I try not to send work home that has not been completely reviewed by the child and myself.

Sometimes I add a more thorough comment. I do want to provide feedback about the way the child has approached the problem. I want to provide validation and confirmation without setting up a system that suggests that my way is the only or right way. Sometimes I simply write a question that I would like to hear answered. I might also just record a question mark because I do not understand the work enough to know what to ask. I find I need to sort the work so that the next day I know which pieces can be returned for revision by the children independently and which children I want to meet with in a small group or individually.

Recently, I've also started putting a line under numbers or letters that have been printed as a reversal. I am always trying to maximize learning opportunities, and I know that practice is important. I hear from parents that my comments and notations are helpful. I know they do not always understand the work that is coming home because it looks so different from what they remember from their own primary education. Sometimes I include an explanatory paragraph about the investigation or problem and I attach this to the work that goes home. These brief comments can set a context that allows a family member to view a child's work with more understanding. Sometimes I attach a more general note that can act as a conduit for conversation at home (see Figure 9–1).

How Can I Share Show-and-Tell with Parents/Families?

Parents are their child's first teachers, and we need to acknowledge their important role. Just like anything else that happens in the school life of a child, we have a responsibility to share it with

---

We have been working with story problems for the past two weeks. Attached is the work your child has completed. I am very proud of the efforts I see. You might want to:

1. Ask your child to tell you about this work.
2. Pick a problem (or two) and ask your child what it was about and how he or she solved it.
3. Try to solve one of the problems, or a similar problem, together.

In school I am always looking for work that shows careful thought and an understanding of the problem and the solution. This class is working very hard during math time. I hope you see the growth your child is making in this area.

FIGURE 9–1   *Teacher's note attached to work sent home*

their families. Some teachers invite parents to take part in math class as a volunteer or observer. In this way, parents can see first-hand what and how their children are learning math. Other teachers send home newsletters that capture some of the sights and sounds of the classroom, including significant moments that involve mathematics.

As mentioned in the previous teacher reflection, writing individualized notes on a paper or attaching a brief description of the purpose and/or outcomes of an investigation also help to keep families informed. At conference time or in a report form, including examples of things we have learned about their child from classroom conversations and the child's recorded work can be very powerful. Nothing speaks louder to parents than their children's own words, actions, and products.

Are There Checklists That Can Help Me Consider My Students' Work from a Show-and-Tell Perspective?

It is helpful to think about a checklist or rubric that one either reviews when considering student work or internalizes as part of daily teaching. Here are some questions to keep in mind.

When telling:

- How comfortable are students when they speak to each other and the teacher, in a small or large group?
- How often does the student engage in the act of telling?
- Can I understand what is being shared? Can the student's peers understand?
- Does the student consider the audience when speaking?
- Do the students respond to each other's comments?
- Does the vocabulary the student uses match classroom norms? Traditional terminology?
- Are the student's comments mathematically correct?

When showing:

- Is the student's representation accurate?
- Does the student use representation as a strategy to understand and solve the problem?
- Does the student represent the way he or she solves the problem?

- Does the student's representation include an answer to the problem?
- Can the student explain his or her representation?
- Can the student represent ideas in more than one way?
- Does the student use several forms of representation?
- Can the student understand the representations of others?
- Is the student's representation mathematically correct?

When using a show-and-tell approach, we must also consider equity. Checklists can be developed that help note the frequency of who is sharing. Does one child dominate the conversation? Is one child's work always being used as a model? Conversely, does one child rarely speak? Is one child's work rarely shown? We must be proactive in ensuring that all students have equal access to showing and telling. Everyone's ideas and work are valid and need validating.

How Do I Get Started?

Any time we try something new, we need to give ourselves permission to fumble around a bit. We need to find our level of comfort or threshold for tolerance of new behaviors. Teachers of today's rigorous agendas need to find a balance. There is a great deal to teach and learn in K–2 classrooms.

We also need to examine our attitudes to make sure that they support a show-and-tell environment. A group of teachers participating in a workshop about the show-and-tell approach made a poster to help them remember their goals (see Figure 9–2).

The following teacher reflection reminds us of how complex this work can be and of the time and energy it takes to help children show and tell their ideas.

Teacher Reflection

When I taught second grade last year, I would typically ask students to solve a math problem and to "show their thinking using pictures, numbers, and/or words."

My students did not come from first grades where such a thing was ever asked of them, and so it took a while for most of them to figure out what I meant by

> *To support a classroom where my students show and tell their thinking and become proficient users of mathematics, I will:*
>
> - Be curious about my students' learning and thinking
> - Believe that my students' work is of mathematical value
> - Take time for students to share their work with each other
> - Enjoy the variety with which my students process, communicate, and represent their ideas
> - Monitor my students' conceptual understanding
> - Determine the mathematical validity of my students' different responses
> - Use student work to inform my instructional decisions and my assessment strategies

FIGURE 9–2 *Poster made by teachers*

my request. I had to work with them to think about how they solved mental arithmetic problems, and how to say how they solved them, and then how to write or draw a representation of their thought processes.

Once they were more or less up and running with the idea of "how did you solve it and how can you show that on paper?" I saw, naturally, a lot of variety. There were children who used direct modeling with Unifix cubes or tally marks (or highly detailed drawings of icons, such as cats with whiskers, stripes, collars, names, and so on). For some of them, the recording and the solving was the same step, because they drew their tallies or kitties in order to solve the problem, and performed their operation right on their representation. Students who used cubes either drew their cubes and somehow represented the mathematical action (crossing out, circling), or else they wrote a narrative such as "I got 25 cubes and took away 7 and the answer is 18." There was also fairly often a less mathematically detailed "I used cubes" or "I counted on my fingers."

Students who took numbers apart and put them back together, or performed a series of steps, used many different ways to show their thoughts. Many would list a series of steps. Many would draw lines between numbers or parts of numbers and write partial sums. Again, some would write a narrative, "Well, I know 30 + 30 is 60, so then I added . . ."

Ideas for how to record definitely developed in interesting ways, and in ways similar to how problem-solving strategies developed. Sometimes a student would develop or adopt a way of recording that would become "Rachel's way." Students would try each other's ways, and the methods I modeled at the board. I, in turn, modeled ways that came from students and ways that were mine that I thought would be helpful to some students.

Sometimes students' representations reflected how they actually solved the problem, and sometimes they did not. I would listen to a student talk through a strategy involving decomposing a number or thinking about groups of ten, and then the paper would show tally marks not arranged in groups, as if the student had counted by ones.

Sometimes the recording would be part of the actual solving—for example, a student would record steps as the problem was being solved. Sometimes the student would solve the problem without making a mark on the paper and then do some drawing and writing.

At all times, I tried to help my students focus on the purpose of recording in the same way I tried to accentuate the importance of having multiple strategies. Their recordings may not have always matched their strategies but their level of awareness and their ability to share this with others continued to evolve all year.

As we focus on students' thinking about mathematics and set high expectations for both them and ourselves, there is much to see and hear. Countless opportunities arise for rich mathematics and sound learning. When students show and tell, those opportunities are maximized, and important mathematical concepts and skills are internalized and understood. As written on a poster hanging in one classroom:

> When I show and tell . . . I can see and hear what I
> think.
> When I show and tell . . . I can understand.
> When I show and tell . . . I can take pride in what I've
> learned.
> When I show and tell . . . I can share what I think with
> others and learn from them.

When teachers help children to show and tell, there is much to celebrate!

References

Atkinson, Sue. 1992. *Mathematics with Reason.* Portsmouth, NH: Heinemann.

Baratta-Lorton, Mary. 1976. *Mathematics Their Way.* Menlo Park, CA: Addison-Wesley.

Burns, Marilyn. 2000. *About Teaching Mathematics: A K–8 Resource.* 2d ed. Sausalito, CA: Math Solutions Publications.

Carle, Eric. 1995. *Walter the Baker.* New York: Simon and Schuster for Young Readers.

Carpenter, Thomas, Elizabeth Fennema, Megan Franke, Linda Levi, and Susan Empson. 1999. *Children's Mathematics: Cognitively Guided Instruction.* Portsmouth, NH: Heinemann.

Casey, M. Beth, Ronald Nuttall, and Elizabeth Pezaris. 2001. "Spatial-Mechanical Reasoning Skills Versus Mathematics Self-Confidence as Mediators of Gender Differences on Mathematics Subtests Using Cross-National Gender-Based Items." *Journal for Research in Mathematics Education* 32 (January): 28–57.

Clements, Douglas. 2000. "Young Children's Ideas About Geometric Shapes." *Teaching Children Mathematics* 6 (April): 482–488.

Clements, Douglas, and Julie Meredith. 1998. *Shapes—Making Shapes.* Palo Alto, CA: Dale Seymour Publications.

Corwin, Rebecca. 1996. *Talking Mathematics: Supporting Children's Voices.* Portsmouth, NH: Heinemann.

Crews, Donald. *Ten Black Dots.* 1968. New York: Greenwillow Books.

Cuoco, Albert, and Frances Curcio, eds. 2001. *The Roles of Representation in School Mathematics 2001 Yearbook.* Reston, VA: National Council of Teachers of Mathematics.

Dacey Schulman, Linda, and Rebeka Eston. 1999. *Growing Mathematical Ideas in Kindergarten.* Sausalito, CA: Math Solutions Publications.

Dodds, Dayle Ann. 1994. *The Shapes of Things.* Cambridge, MA: Candlewick Press.

Economopoulos, Karen, and Susan Jo Russell. 1998. *Investigations in Number, Data, and Space: Counting Ourselves and Others.* Developed by TERC in Cambridge, MA. Menlo Park, CA: Dale Seymour Publications.

Fennell, Francis ("Skip"), and Tom Robbins. 2001. "Representation: An Important Process for Teaching and Learning Mathematics." *Teaching Children Mathematics* 7 (January): 288–293.

Greenes, Carole. 1999. "Ready to Learn: Developing Young Children's Mathematical Powers." In *Mathematics in the Early Years*, edited by Juanita Copley, pp. 39–47. Reston, VA: National Council of Teachers of Mathematics, and Washington, D.C.: National Association for the Education of Young Children.

Greeno, James, and Roger Hall. 1997. "Practicing Representation: Learning with and About Representational Forms." *Phi Delta Kappan* 79 (January): 361–367.

Hellen, Nancy. 1998. *The Bus Stop.* New York: Orchard Books.

Hiebert, James, Thomas Carpenter, Elizabeth Fennema, Karen Furson, Dianna Wearne, Hanlie Murray, Alwyn Olivier, and Piet Human. 1998. *Making Sense: Teaching and Learning Mathematics with Understanding.* Portsmouth, NH: Heinemann.

Kamaii, Constance, and Leslie Baker Houseman. 1999. *Young Children Reinvent Arithmetic: Implication of Piaget's Theory.* 2d ed. New York: Teachers College Press.

Kliman, Marlene, and Susan Jo Russell. 1998. *Investigations in Number, Data, and Space: Building Number Sense.* Developed by TERC in Cambridge, MA. Menlo Park, CA: Dale Seymour Publications.

McCloskey, Robert. 1941. *Make Way for Ducklings.* New York: Viking Press.

Mills, Heidi, Timothy O'Keefe, and David Whitin. 1996. *Mathematics in the Making.* Portsmouth, NH: Heinemann.

Myler, Rolf. 1962. *How Big Is a Foot?* New York: Dell Publishing.

National Council of Teachers of Mathematics (NCTM). 2000. *Principles and Standards for School Mathematics.* Reston, VA: NCTM.

Parkes, Brenda, Judith Smith, and Mary Davy. 1997. *The Enormous Watermelon.* Crystal Lake, IL: Rigby.

Pratt, Chris, and Alison Garton. 1993. *Systems of Representation in Children: Development and Use.* New York: John Wiley and Sons.

Robbins, Ken. 1990. *A Flower Grows.* New York: Dial.

Russell, Susan Jo. 2000. "Developing Computational Fluency with Whole Numbers." *Teaching Children Mathematics* 6 (November): 154–158.

Schulman, Linda, and Rebeka Eston. 1998. "A Problem Worth Revisiting." *Teaching Children Mathematics* 5 (October): 72–77.

Whitin, Phyllis, and David Whitin. 2000. *Math Is Language Too: Talking and Writing in the Mathematics Classroom.* Urbana, IL: National Council of Teachers of English.

Yackel, Erna. 1997. "A Foundation for Algebraic Reasoning in the Early Years." *Teaching Children Mathematics* 3 (February): 276–281.